KEY TO SYMBOLS

$\sqrt{x}$	Math		People in History
	Science & Technology		Inventions & Machines
	Human Body		Exploration & Discovery
	Natural World		Warfare & Weapons
	Scientists at Work		The Arts
	Earth & Space		English Language
	Geography	?	General Knowledge
	History		

You will find more than 1700 questions in this book. If you are answering questions on your own, just cover the answers with your hand or a piece of card. You may want to write down your answers and count up your scores for each quiz.

If you are doing the quizzes with a partner or in teams, unfold the base and stand the Flip Quiz on a flat surface between you and your partner. Read the questions aloud (but not the answers!) and allow your partner to say the answers or write them down. You may answer each question in turn or answer an entire quiz in turn. Keep your scores on a piece of paper and compare results.

The illustrations are there to help you get the right answers when competing with a partner. For instance, if you are answering Quiz 1 questions, you will be looking at and reading out Quiz 2. However, the illustrations you see are clues to help you do Quiz 1. Look at the labels by the illustrations. These tell you which question they are clues for. The pictures behind the quiz numbers at the top of the page are not such obvious clues, but they may still help you get an answer.

The questions are divided into fifteen subjects: Math, Science & Technology, Human Body, Natural World, Scientists at Work, Earth & Space, Geography, History, People in History, Inventions & Machines, Exploration & Discovery, Warfare & Weapons, The Arts, English Language, and General Knowledge.

As you progress through the quizzes, you will notice that the questions get a little harder. We think the easiest level is Level 1 and the hardest is Level 3, but you may find it the other way around. It all depends on what you happen to know.

Levels
There are three levels of question; they get harder as you progress.

Question categories
The questions are divided into 15 subjects (see key above).

Picture clues 1
These visual clues are not always obvious (and they don't have labels).

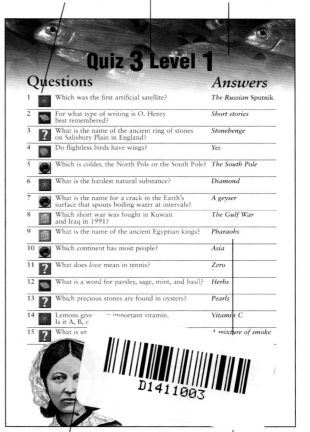

Picture clues 2
These visual clues will often help you get the answer; the label tells you which question they refer to.

Answers
When doing the quizzes on your own, cover the answers with your hand or a piece of paper.

Quiz 1 Level 1

Questions

Answers

		Question	Answer
1		What is the name for a straight line that joins one corner of a square to the opposite corner?	*A diagonal*
2		Looking toward a ship's bow, is the port side on the left or the right?	*The left side*
3		What type of shellfish is usually used to make chowder?	*Clam*
4		Who was Sherlock Holmes's assistant?	*Dr. Watson*
5		Is the Sun mainly solid, like the Earth, or liquid or gas?	*Gas (mostly hydrogen)*
6		What is the name for a large, slow-moving mass of ice on the surface of the land?	*A glacier*
7		What is the national bird of New Zealand?	*The kiwi*
8		What word describes a family or species of animals that has died out?	*Extinct*
9		Who became U.S. President when Abraham Lincoln was assassinated?	*Andrew Johnson*
10		Which tree is the most massive?	*A California redwood*
11		Which reptiles ruled the world for more than 160 million years?	*Dinosaurs*
12		What do you call people who study animals?	*Zoologists*
13		Who wrote the music for *The Lion King*?	*Elton John*
14		Which is the Red Planet?	*Mars*
15		Where is the Grand Canyon, the world's longest gorge?	*Arizona*

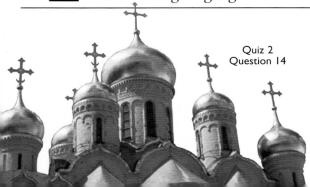

Quiz 2
Question 14

Quiz 2
Question 4

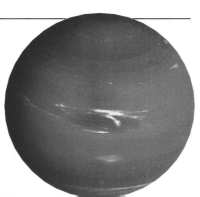

Quiz 2 Level 1

Questions   ## Answers

#	Question	Answer
1	What country's flag is a red circle on a white background?	Japan
2	What does R.S.V.P. mean on an invitation?	Please reply
3	What is the capital of India?	New Delhi
4	Which planet is named after the Roman god of the sea?	Neptune
5	How many corners does a cube have?	8
6	What is a vertebrate?	An animal that has a backbone
7	Where are the lands of the midnight sun?	The Arctic and Antarctic
8	Who is the patron saint of Ireland?	Saint Patrick
9	Who was the first man on the Moon?	Neil Armstrong
10	Which Viking landed in North America nearly 500 years before Columbus?	Leif Erikson
11	What does an entomologist study?	Insects
12	How many limbs does an octopus have?	8
13	Which is the noun in this sentence: *The bird is black*?	Bird
14	What is another name for a cupola?	A dome
15	What is the square root of 64?	8

Quiz I
Question I1

Quiz I
Question I4

Quiz 3 Level 1

		Questions	Answers
1		Which was the first artificial satellite?	*The Russian* Sputnik
2		For what type of writing is O. Henry best remembered?	*Short stories*
3		What is the name of the ancient ring of stones on Salisbury Plain in England?	*Stonehenge*
4		Do flightless birds have wings?	*Yes*
5		Which is colder, the North Pole or the South Pole?	*The South Pole*
6		What is the hardest natural substance?	*Diamond*
7		What is the name for a crack in the Earth's surface that spouts boiling water at intervals?	*A geyser*
8		Which short war was fought in Kuwait and Iraq in 1991?	*The Gulf War*
9		What is the name of the ancient Egyptian kings?	*Pharaohs*
10		Which continent has the most people?	*Asia*
11		What does *love* mean in tennis?	*Zero*
12		What is a word for parsley, sage, mint, and basil?	*Herbs*
13		Which precious stones are found in oysters?	*Pearls*
14		Lemons give us an important vitamin. Is it A, B, or C?	*Vitamin C*
15		What is smog?	*A mixture of smoke and fog*

Quiz 4
Question 10

Quiz 4
Question 11

Quiz 4 Level 1

Questions

Answers

#		Question	Answer
1		Which Italian traveler wrote a famous account of life in the Far East?	*Marco Polo*
2		What is an alloy?	*A mixture of two or more metals*
3		Who wrote the *Alice in Wonderland* stories?	*Lewis Carroll*
4		What is an invertebrate?	*An animal that lacks a backbone*
5		What is the smallest piece of a substance that can exist on its own?	*A molecule*
6		Was Leonardo da Vinci a general, a politician, or an artist?	*A great Italian artist*
7		In which sport would you use a foil?	*Fencing*
8		What does a marine biologist study?	*Sea life*
9		What is the capital of Wales?	*Cardiff*
10		Who was known as the "Lady with the Lamp"?	*Florence Nightingale*
11		Is a tomato a fruit or a vegetable?	*A fruit (it has seeds)*
12		What is 10 percent of 80?	*8*
13		Which river flows through London?	*Thames River*
14		Who wrote *The Red Badge of Courage*?	*Stephen Crane*
15		What is a young deer called?	*A fawn*

Quiz 3
Question 1

Quiz 3
Question 12

Quiz 5 Level 1

1		Where is the Great Barrier Reef?	*Off the northeastern coast of Australia*
2		What is the name for a picture or design made up of many small pieces of stone or tile?	*A mosaic*
3		Who led the Russian Revolution in 1917 and became the first leader of communist Russia?	*Lenin*
4		In which sport would you use a number 5 iron?	*Golf*
5		Which planet is named after the goddess of love?	*Venus*
6		Where is the world's largest rain forest?	*The Amazon basin in South America*
7		What does a television aerial do?	*Collects television signals*
8		What are stigma, sepals, and anthers part of?	*Flowers*
9		Which scientist thought of gravity when he saw an apple fall?	*Sir Isaac Newton*
10		How many spots on a pair of dice?	*42*
11		Who founded the Boy Scouts?	*Sir Robert Baden-Powell*
12		What does *never say die* mean?	*Never give up hope*
13		What is the name for an animal that feeds on refuse or the flesh of dead animals?	*A scavenger*
14		Where would you find a delta?	*At the mouth of a river*
15		What is a female lion called?	*A lioness*

Quiz 6
Question 3

Quiz 6
Question 9

Quiz 6
Question 12

Quiz 6 Level 1

#		Question	Answer
1		What is a dictator?	*A ruler who has total power*
2		In which war was the Battle of the Somme?	*World War I*
3		What plant that has white berries can you kiss under at Christmas?	*Mistletoe*
4		In which continent are the Andes Mountains?	*South America*
5		What in the common name for a poisonous mushroom?	*A toadstool*
6		Do seaweeds have roots?	*No (they cling to stones, shells, etc.)*
7		What is a planet?	*A large mass that orbits a star*
8		Which French military leader is usually shown with one hand inside his coat?	*Napoleon Bonaparte*
9		Can the kiwi bird fly?	*No*
10		What is the name for a space that is completely empty of air and everything else?	*A vacuum*
11		Which is higher: a baritone or a tenor?	*A tenor*
12		What did Thomas Edison invent to help us move on from gaslight?	*The light bulb*
13		Which country did England fight in the Hundred Years' War?	*France*
14		How many sides does a parallelogram have?	*4*
15		Which river flows through New Orleans?	*Mississippi*

Quiz 5
Question 11

Quiz 5
Question 10

Quiz 7 Level 1

#	Question	Answer
1	Which international organization was founded to care for soldiers wounded in war?	*The Red Cross*
2	What does *beauty is skin deep* mean?	*You can't judge things by appearance*
3	Loggerhead and snapping are types of what?	*Turtles*
4	Which country's flag has a white cross?	*Switzerland*
5	What is the study of acoustics?	*The study of sound*
6	Which countries make up the Iberian Peninsula?	*Spain and Portugal*
7	Where does cork come from?	*From the bark of a tree (the cork oak)*
8	What is the main difference between algebra and arithmetic?	*Algebra uses letters to stand for numbers*
9	In which war was the Battle of Gettysburg fought?	*The U.S. Civil War*
10	Which European country has borders with France, Germany, Austria, and Italy?	*Switzerland*
11	What are the Common Blue, Peacock, and Swallowtail?	*Types of butterfly*
12	What does VE Day stand for?	*Victory in Europe Day*
13	A diamond is a crystal. True or false?	*True*
14	Who was the first person to reach the South Pole?	*Roald Amundsen*
15	What is the name of the person who directs an orchestra?	*The conductor*

Quiz 8
Question 10

Quiz 8
Question 12

Quiz 8 Level 1

#		Question	Answer
1		Which painter cut off his own ear?	*Vincent Van Gogh*
2		To which country do Majorca and Minorca belong?	*Spain*
3		What is the word *bus* short for?	*Omnibus*
4		Which creatures did St. Patrick drive out of Ireland?	*Snakes*
5		Which continent are the islands of the the Caribbean part of?	*North America*
6		Which ships brought Columbus's sailors from Spain to America?	*Niña, Pinta, and Santa María*
7		How many degrees in a circle?	*360*
8		What does the abbreviation R.B.I. stand for in baseball?	*Runs Batted In*
9		Which is the largest country in South America?	*Brazil*
10		Which American President said *Read my lips*?	*George H.W. Bush*
11		What is the name for the loosely draped tunic worn by the Romans?	*The toga*
12		What are Jerseys, Herefords, and Shorthorns?	*Breeds of cattle*
13		Which woman scientist won two Nobel Prizes?	*Marie Curie (in 1903 and 1911)*
14		How do the British spell *center*?	*Centre*
15		What is the smallest part of a substance?	*An atom*

Quiz 7
Question 6

Quiz 7
Question 14

Quiz 9 Level 1

Questions

Answers

#	Question	Answer
1	In which city is the Arc de Triomphe?	*Paris*
2	What are Mandarins, Mallards, and Eiders?	*Types of duck*
3	Who started the Free French Movement in Britain during World War II?	*General de Gaulle*
4	What is the name of the tube that takes food from your mouth to your stomach?	*The esophagus or gullet*
5	Who wrote a book called *On the Origin of Species*?	*Charles Darwin*
6	What is the Earth's solid outer layer called?	*The crust*
7	Two of the Brontë sisters were Charlotte and Anne. Who was the third?	*Emily*
8	Which composer continued to compose great music when he was totally deaf?	*Ludwig van Beethoven*
9	How many sides does a hexagon have?	*6*
10	Which is the largest city in Africa?	*Cairo*
11	Which London bridge opens to let ships through?	*Tower Bridge*
12	What English word is made from the words for two Greek letters, *alpha* and *beta*?	*Alphabet*
13	What is a cosmonaut?	*A Russian astronaut*
14	What do butterflies use their antennae for?	*To smell*
15	How did Joan of Arc die?	*She was burned at the stake*

Quiz 10
Question 6

Quiz 10
Question 8

Quiz 10 Level 1

Questions

Answers

#	Question	Answer
1	Which Christian church has most members?	*The Roman Catholic*
2	What is the capital of Sri Lanka?	*Colombo*
3	How many degrees are there in a right angle?	*90 degrees*
4	Who flew the first powered airplane?	*The Wright brothers*
5	Which center of filmmaking is in Los Angeles?	*Hollywood*
6	Who was president of the United States during the Civil War?	*Abraham Lincoln*
7	What are layers of coal called?	*Seams*
8	Buff Orpingtons, Leghorns, and Rhode Island Reds are all types of what?	*Chickens*
9	What are crabs, lobsters, and shrimp?	*They are shellfish (crustaceans)*
10	Which unit of measurement uses the distance light travels in one year—9,470,000,000,000 km?	*A light year*
11	Who in 1961 was the first person to travel into space?	*The Russian Yuri Gagarin*
12	What is an antonym?	*A word that means the opposite*
13	Who was the second President of the United States?	*John Adams*
14	How do grasshoppers make a noise?	*By rubbing their back legs together*
15	What does *armistice* mean?	*An end to fighting*

Quiz 9
Question 2

Quiz 9
Question 8

Quiz 11 Level 1

	Questions	Answers
1	In which city is Fenway Park?	*Boston*
2	The Channel Tunnel links which two countries?	*The United Kingdom and France*
3	Which part of an egg is used to make mayonnaise?	*The yolk*
4	When archeologists dig a site, what is it called?	*An excavation*
5	How many seconds are there in an hour?	*3,600*
6	What is an accurate seagoing clock called?	*A chronometer*
7	In which country are Rio de Janeiro and São Paulo?	*Brazil*
8	Which great Austrian composer wrote over 600 pieces of music, including many famous operas?	*Wolfgang Amadeus Mozart*
9	Which is the second-heaviest land animal?	*The hippopotamus*
10	What is the capital of Hungary?	*Budapest*
11	Who was the famous leader of the Huns?	*Attila*
12	Are mammals warm- or cold-blooded?	*Warm-blooded*
13	Which American civil rights leader was assassinated in 1968?	*Martin Luther King*
14	Which four-sided shape has equal sides and equal angles?	*A square*
15	What does *allegiance* mean?	*Loyalty*

Quiz 12
Question 10

Quiz 12
Question 11

Quiz 12 Level 1

Questions

Answers

		Questions	Answers
1		Which country has borders with France, Germany, and the Netherlands?	*Belgium*
2		Which soft-bodied group of animals includes snails, slugs, oysters, and octopuses?	*Mollusks*
3		In which ocean is the island of Mauritius?	*The Indian Ocean*
4		What does *sarcastic* mean?	*Mocking and scornful*
5		In which city are the main administrative offices of the European Union?	*Brussels*
6		What is the name of the disorder of the blood caused by having too few red blood cells?	*Anemia*
7		Bees don't have to learn to sting; they do it by what?	*Instinct*
8		Which country invaded Kuwait in 1990?	*Iraq*
9		Which country celebrates Guy Fawkes Day?	*The United Kingdom*
10		Which empire specialized in building straight roads and bridges?	*The Roman*
11		What is an anemometer?	*A wind-gauge*
12		What is the capital of Mexico?	*Mexico City*
13		Who were known as Tommies?	*British soldiers (in World War I)*
14		For what is Gregor Mendel famous?	*For his work on heredity*
15		What do you call the coat of a sheep?	*Fleece*

Quiz 11
Question 3

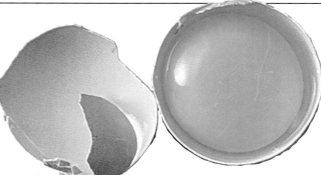

Quiz 13 Level 1

Questions

Answers

#	Question	Answer
1	Which continent did Mary Kingsley explore?	*Africa*
2	Which country did Germany invade in September 1939?	*Poland*
3	Who wrote "America the Beautiful"?	*Katherine Lee Bates*
4	Who was the first woman in space?	*Valentina Tereshkova (USSR, in 1963)*
5	With what invention is the name of Gillette associated?	*The safety razor*
6	The Northrop f-5 "Freedom fighter" saw service in which war: World War II or the Vietnam War?	*Vietnam War*
7	What was the name of the giant statue that once stood at the entrance of Rhodes harbor?	*The Colossus*
8	When was the battle of Bunker Hill: 1755, 1765, or 1775?	*1775*
9	What do we call a picture carved from a flat stone, as were produced by ancient people?	*A relief*
10	What medical first did Christiaan Barnard of South Africa achieve in 1967?	*First heart transplant*
11	Which animals did armies in India and Cambodia use like tanks?	*Elephants*
12	In which city is there a famous opera house with sail-like roofs, opened in 1973?	*Sydney, Australia*
13	Samuel Pepys is remembered for writing what?	*His diary (1660 – 1669)*
14	To make a spark, what must flint be struck against?	*Iron*
15	In what sport was Joe Louis a world champion?	*Boxing*

Quiz 14
Question 11

Quiz 14
Question 15

Quiz 14 Level 1

Questions

		Answers
1	Where did Joshua Slocum sail from 1895 to 1898?	*Around the world (first person to do this alone)*
2	Which Greek hero could only be wounded in his heels?	*Achilles*
3	In which war was radar first used?	*World War II (1939-1945)*
4	What was the name of the Scottish hero in the film *Braveheart*?	*William Wallace*
5	In which Indian city did Mother Teresa do her good works?	*Calcutta*
6	Which Christian saint is famous for his love of animals?	*St. Francis of Assisi (1182-1226)*
7	Who won the Six-Day War of 1967?	*Israel*
8	Which Tudor warship was raised from the seabed and is now preserved in Portsmouth, England?	*The* **Mary Rose**
9	Which land did Cartier claim for France in 1534?	*Canada*
10	In which story do Captain Nemo and the submarine *Nautilus* appear?	**Twenty Thousand Leagues under the Sea**
11	Which of King Henry VIII's wives was mother of Queen Elizabeth I?	*Anne Boleyn*
12	Was the Arab Ibn Battuta a famous traveler or a famous doctor?	*A famous traveler*
13	The artist Canaletto painted many views of which Italian city?	*Venice*
14	What word meaning "sudden fear" is derived from the name of the Greek god Pan?	*Panic*
15	Which Egyptian pharaoh's tomb was discovered in 1922?	*Tutankhamun*

Quiz 13
Question 5

Quiz 13
Question 6

Quiz 15 Level 1

Questions

Answers

		Questions	Answers
1		Which area was known as "Seward's Folly" when the U.S. bought it in 1867?	*Alaska*
2		Which English king tried to make the tide obey him to show how powerless he was?	*King Canute (Cnut)*
3		What do we call the illustrations which Celtic monks used to adorn religious works?	*Illuminations*
4		What happened to the Japanese cities of Hiroshima and Nagasaki in August 1945?	*They were destroyed by atomic bombs*
5		Who led a revolution in Cuba in 1959?	*Fidel Castro*
6		Where is Dunkirk, from where over 300,000 service men were evacuated in World War II?	*Northern France*
7		In which country was the medical treatment called acupuncture developed?	*China*
8		By what name was Martha Canary better known in the Wild West?	*Calamity Jane*
9		What branch of mathematics did the ancient Egyptians develop when building the pyramids?	*Geometry*
10		Where is the North West Passage, discovered in 1906 by Roald Amundsen?	*Around Canada. It links the Atlantic and Pacific*
11		The people of which country worshiped the gods Amun and Osiris: Mexico, Egypt, or Greece?	*Egypt*
12		Which American frontiersman was killed at the Battle of the Alamo in 1836?	*Davy Crockett*
13		What kind of triangular sail invented in about AD500 allowed ships to sail more into the wind?	*The lateen sail*
14		Which ancient Indian religion strictly forbids its followers from harming any living thing?	*Jainism*
15		Who wrote the poem *The Charge of the Light Brigade*?	*Alfred Tennyson*

Quiz 16
Question 12

Quiz 16
Question 2

Quiz 16
Question 4

Quiz 16 Level 1

Questions

Answers

#		Question	Answer
1		Which U.S. airman flew over both the North and South Poles?	*Richard E. Byrd*
2		Which king sent the Spanish Armada to war against England in 1588?	*Philip II*
3		By what name is the French king Charles the Great better known?	*Charlemagne*
4		What was a Dutchman named Hans Lippershey the first to look through in about 1600?	*The telescope*
5		What did Robert Bunsen invent?	*A gas burner (used in laboratories)*
6		When was the first airmail postal service introduced: 1911, 1921, or 1931?	*1911 (across London)*
7		What nationality was the composer Sibelius?	*Finnish*
8		Which calendar starts 3,760 years before the birth of Jesus Christ?	*The Jewish calendar*
9		Which U.S. president was a famous general during World War II?	*Eisenhower*
10		What did Robert Watson-Watt invent in the 1930s?	*Radar*
11		What kind of armor did Norman knights wear?	*Chain-mail*
12		Before the invention of pens, what was a feather called when it was trimmed and used for writing?	*A quill*
13		Who was the first European to sail round the Cape of Good Hope?	*Bartolomeu Dias (Portugal)*
14		Which British poet died in Greece in 1824?	*Byron*
15		Which British king spoke German but hardly any English?	*George I*

Quiz 15
Question 11

Quiz 15
Question 3

Quiz 17 Level 1

Questions

Answers

#	Question	Answer
1	What nationality was atom scientist Niels Bohr?	*Danish*
2	Which king ruled England, Denmark, and Norway at the same time?	*Canute (or Cnut)*
3	Where was the great gold rush of 1849?	*California*
4	How many astronauts have stood on the Moon: two, eight, or twelve?	*Twelve*
5	What crop did Jimmy Carter grow before he became U.S. president?	*Peanuts*
6	After whom is the Bering Strait named?	*Danish explorer Vitus Bering*
7	Which two important metals were mined in England during Roman times?	*Lead and tin*
8	Which science-fiction story on radio caused a panic in the USA in 1938?	The War of the Worlds
9	In which Asian country was the Khmer empire founded in about AD900?	*Cambodia*
10	Which British prime minister had the forenames Margaret Hilda?	*Margaret Thatcher*
11	Did Mongol soldiers drink horse's milk, coffee, or pineapple juice?	*Horse's milk*
12	Was the first globe of the Earth made in 1350, 1492, or 1796?	*1492*
13	Which fireworks-styled weapons were first used in China?	*Rockets*
14	What were the pyramid-like platforms built in ancient Mesopotamia called?	*Ziggurats*
15	Which metal made Andrew Carnegie's millions?	*Steel*

Quiz 18
Question 8

Quiz 18
Question 7

Quiz 18
Question 5

Quiz 18 Level 1

Questions

Answers

1	In which continent are the Atlas Mountains?	*Africa*
2	Michael Collins was a famous revolutionary: in which country?	*Ireland*
3	Is Verdi's *Nabucco* a disease, an opera, or a rare African bird?	*An opera*
4	Which country does Edam cheese come from?	*The Netherlands (Holland)*
5	What is the large medieval catapult that was used to attack castles called?	*Trebuchet*
6	Which Roman god was ruler of the Underworld?	*Pluto*
7	In which country did samurai warriors live?	*Japan*
8	Which 1947 invention made pocket-sized radios possible?	*The transistor*
9	A famous thriller writer wrote a children's book called *Chitty Chitty Bang Bang*—who was he?	*Ian Fleming*
10	Who won the sea battle of Sluys in 1346?	*The English (beating the French)*
11	In which Shakespeare play does a prince of Denmark see his father's ghost?	**Hamlet**
12	What year was the first digital computer built: 1930, 1946, or 1965?	*1946*
13	Which messy friend of Charlie Brown always appeared with a cloud of dust?	*Pigpen*
14	Which oath, taken by modern doctors, is named after a Greek physician?	*The Hippocratic oath (after Hippocrates)*
15	How many kings of England have been called Henry?	*Eight*

Quiz 17
Question 12

Quiz 17
Question 8

Quiz 19 Level 1

Questions

Answers

1		Which U.S. Army unit did Custer lead at the Little Big Horn?	*The 7th Cavalry*
2		Which real-life Tudor inspired a play and a film called *A Man for all Seasons*?	*Sir Thomas More*
3		Which river in Africa did 19th-century explorers strive to find the source of?	*The Nile*
4		Which bridge in London, completed in 1894, can open and close?	*Tower Bridge*
5		Which Israelite leader was ordered by God to kill his son Isaac?	*Abraham*
6		What prehistoric works of art were found in caves at Lascaux, France?	*Wall paintings*
7		What did Balboa see for the first time in 1513?	*The Pacific Ocean (first European to see it)*
8		Who made the first mass-produced car, the Model-T?	*Henry Ford*
9		Which number did the ancient Babylonians use as a unit for measuring time and angles?	*60*
10		Which islands was Magellan visiting when he was killed in a fight between rival tribes?	*The Philippines*
11		Was the *Turtle* of 1778 an early submarine, a primitive tank, or a rocket?	*An early submarine*
12		In 1971 East Pakistan became an independent country. What was it called?	*Bangladesh*
13		Which great Muslim leader made peace with the Crusaders in 1192?	*Saladin*
14		Which country was the first to introduce the metric system of weights and measures in 1795?	*France*
15		What emblem did a Crusader knight wear?	*A red cross*

Quiz 20
Question 13

Quiz 20
Question 6

Quiz 20
Question 7

Quiz 20 Level 1

Questions

Answers

1	How many countries were founder members of the European Community in 1957?	*Six*
2	What was built across the United States in 1869?	*The first coast to coast railroad*
3	Who sent Lewis and Clark on their expedition?	*President Thomas Jefferson*
4	Which German composer, born in 1685, wrote *The Messiah* and the *Water Music*?	*Handel*
5	Who were supposed to obey the laws of chivalry?	*Medieval knights*
6	How many years ago did the first modern humans appear?	*150,000 years ago*
7	Who wrote *Little Women*?	*Louisa May Alcott*
8	Who won the battle of Austerlitz in 1805?	*The French, led by Napoleon*
9	Which continent did Burke and Wills explore?	*Australia*
10	Which jazz musician was known as Satchmo?	*Louis Armstrong*
11	Which Greek city-state fought against Athens in the Peloponnesian war?	*Sparta*
12	Which ancient Greek hero led the expedition of the Argonauts?	*Jason*
13	Which could fire farther: a longbow or a crossbow?	*A longbow*
14	Were Ginger Rogers and Fred Astaire a famous film dance team, comedians, or cartoon characters?	*A film dance team*
15	After which Greek god was the American manned Moon-landing spacecraft named?	*Apollo*

Quiz 19
Question 11

Quiz 19
Question 8

Quiz 19
Question 13

Quiz 21 Level 1

Questions   ## Answers

#	Question	Answer
1	In which country could you watch a kabuki play?	*Japan*
2	What was Thor Heyerdahl's boat *Ra* made from: reeds, ice, or oil drums?	*Reeds*
3	What was the very first kind of aircraft?	*A kite*
4	Which saint do we now call Santa Claus?	*St. Nicholas*
5	When was the Great Fire of London?	*1666*
6	What did Vesalius study in the 1500s?	*Human anatomy— how the body worked*
7	Who was Jesse James?	*A famous outlaw*
8	The people of which country devised our modern numerals?	*India*
9	King Edward III of England had a famous warrior son: what was he called?	*The Black Prince*
10	What were the main weapons on Admiral Nelson's ship the *Victory*?	*Cannons*
11	What did Tycho Brahe of Denmark study?	*The stars*
12	What were Shermans and Grants in World War II?	*Tanks*
13	What invention of the early Middle Ages helped soldiers to fight on horseback?	*The stirrup*
14	What name did the Celts give to their poets?	*Bards*
15	Of which country was Jomo Kenyatta leader?	*Kenya*

Quiz 22
Question 11

Quiz 22
Question 1

Quiz 22 Level 1

Questions

Answers

		Questions	Answers
1		In what sort of boats did the Vikings travel?	*Longships*
2		Which American composer wrote *Rhapsody in Blue*?	*George Gershwin*
3		Which was invented first: the microscope or the telescope?	*The microscope*
4		Which civil rights leader was killed by James Earl Ray in 1968?	*Martin Luther King*
5		What oil-bearing substance did Noah use to coat the Ark and make it waterproof?	*Pitch*
6		Which Italian scientist is said to have dropped cannon balls from a tower to study how they fell to earth?	*Galileo Galilei*
7		How did the ancient Egyptians make casts to support broken limbs?	*With cloth strips soaked in mud*
8		True or false: knights sometimes wore helmets that they could see out of only by leaning forward?	*True: to protect their eyes while jousting*
9		Caliph Harun al-Rashid of Baghdad featured in which series of eastern stories?	**The Arabian Nights**
10		What is the most famous church designed by Sir Christopher Wren?	*St. Paul's Cathedral*
11		What type of exploding weapon is thrown?	*Hand grenade*
12		Who captured Constantinople in 1453?	*The Turks*
13		What kind of engine did the Greek engineer Hero design in the 1st century AD?	*A steam engine*
14		What name was given to religious images painted for the Byzantine church?	*Icons*
15		How did Blaise Pascal of France make addition faster in the 1640s?	*He made a mechanical calculator*

Quiz 21
Question 7

Quiz 21
Question 10

Quiz 23 Level 1

Questions

Answers

		Question	Answer
1		Which English king signed Magna Carta?	*King John*
2		What law did Archimedes discover in the bath?	*Displacement*
3		Who wrote *Catcher in the Rye?*	*J.D. Salinger*
4		Which scientist published his "laws of motion" in 1687?	*Isaac Newton*
5		Which Russian czar worked in an English shipyard?	*Peter the Great*
6		Which King of Spain married Queen Mary of England?	*King Philip*
7		Which famous leader was nicknamed the "little corporal"?	*Napoleon Bonaparte*
8		What kind of engine did Thomas Savery build in 1698?	*A steam pumping engine*
9		On which ship did the famous mutiny of 1789 happen?	*The Bounty*
10		What animals of the Spanish invaders frightened the Incas?	*Horses*
11		In which country was Adolf Hitler born?	*Austria*
12		Under what name did Samuel Langhorne Clemens become famous as a writer?	*Mark Twain*
13		Which 19th-century rebel leader gave his name to a South American country?	*Simón Bolívar (Bolivia)*
14		Did Jethro Tull make improvements in farming or medicine?	*Farming*
15		How many horses did the Egyptians normally use to pull their battle chariots?	*Two*

Quiz 24
Question 7

Quiz 24
Question 2

Quiz 24
Question 8

Quiz 24 Level 1

Questions	Answers

Questions | **Answers**

1. In 1781 William Herschel spotted a planet: which one? — *Uranus*

2. Which English writer wrote a famous *Dictionary of the English Language*? — *Samuel Johnson*

3. Who was British prime minister at the time of the Falklands War in 1982? — *Margaret Thatcher*

4. When was the wheel invented: 32,000BC, 3200BC, or 320BC? — *3200BC in Sumeria*

5. Of which people was William Tell a national hero? — *The Swiss*

6. How many planets were known before a new one was discovered in 1781? — *Six had been known since ancient times*

7. How many legionaires were there in a *century*? — *Eighty*

8. Which country had a ruler called Ivan the Terrible? — *Russia*

9. What fabric did Wallace Carothers invent? — *Nylon*

10. Was Peter Paul Rubens a famous painter, poet, or dancer? — *Painter (1577-1640)*

11. Which Greek inventor discovered the laws of levers and pulleys? — *Archimedes*

12. In which country did warriors called shoguns rule? — *Japan*

13. In what year was Archduke Franz Ferdinand of Austria assassinated? — *1914*

14. Which country had the first steam railroad? — *Britain (1825)*

15. How old was Mozart when he made his first tour as a performer? — *Six*

Quiz 23
Question 15

Quiz 25 Level 1

Questions

Answers

		Questions	Answers
1		Which layer of the Earth is directly below the crust?	*The mantle*
2		What part of the human body are digits?	*Fingers and toes*
3		Does a stalactite point up or down in a cave?	*Down*
4		What is half the diameter of a circle called?	*The radius*
5		Who would tell us about isobars and anticyclones?	*A meteorologist*
6		A seesaw is an example of what type of machine?	*A lever*
7		Which is the tallest mountain on Earth?	*Mt. Everest*
8		Does salt water freeze at a higher or lower temperature than fresh water?	*Lower*
9		What are the smallest blood vessels called?	*Capillaries*
10		What do we call the long rainy season in India and in some other tropical countries?	*The monsoon*
11		What type of scientist might use a Bunsen burner?	*A chemist*
12		On what type of transportation would you find an aileron?	*An airplane*
13		How do bats find their way around?	*By constantly listening to echoes*
14		What is one half of one sixth?	*One twelfth*
15		Where on the body is the cornea?	*The eye*

Quiz 26
Question 14

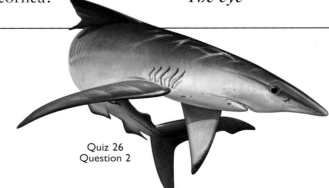

Quiz 26
Question 2

Quiz 26 Level 1

Questions

Answers

		Questions	Answers
1		Cyclones and typhoons are other words for what type of storm?	*Hurricanes*
2		On which part of a shark's body is its dorsal fin?	*Its back*
3		What is the name of the bomb that is launched from a ship to attack a submarine?	*A depth charge*
4		Where is the hard palate?	*The roof of the mouth*
5		You use a pair of what to draw a circle?	*Compasses*
6		What is the name for the explosion that created our universe?	*The Big Bang*
7		What do the British mean when they talk about a gearbox?	*A transmission*
8		What happens to an object if it accelerates?	*Its speed increases*
9		What is a clove hitch?	*A type of knot*
10		Kinetic and potential are types of what?	*Energy*
11		How many half-dozen boxes do you need to collect 40 eggs?	*Seven*
12		What does a paleontologist study?	*Fossils*
13		What is the pampas of South America?	*Vast grasslands*
14		An astrolabe was an earlier version of which device used in navigation?	*A sextant*
15		Where is your sternum?	*Your chest (the breastbone)*

Quiz 25
Question 12

Quiz 25
Question 13

Quiz 27 Level 1

Questions

Answers

1	What type of power is generated by the force of running water?	*Hydroelectric power*
2	What is a ketch?	*A type of sailboat*
3	Within which organs are the alveoli?	*The lungs*
4	If all the angles in a triangle are each 60 degrees, what type of triangle is it?	*An equilateral triangle*
5	If an engineer works out the elevation of something, what has he or she measured?	*Its height above sea level*
6	What do the British mean when they talk about the "bonnet" of a car?	*The hood*
7	What name is given to the curd of milk when it has been squeezed into a solid mass?	*Cheese*
8	What job does a car radiator perform?	*It cools the engine*
9	Which of the following shapes is a quadrilateral: pentagon, triangle, octagon, rectangle?	*Rectangle*
10	What is the name of a group of stars sometimes numbering in their millions?	*A galaxy*
11	On what type of vehicle would you find a derailleur?	*A bicycle*
12	A tremor is a minor form of what event?	*Earthquake*
13	What is 100 divided by eight?	*12.5*
14	What is the name of the tube that supplies nourishment to a baby in its mother's womb?	*The umbilical cord*
15	The Atacama Desert, the driest place on Earth, is on which continent?	*South America*

Quiz 28
Question 2

Quiz 28
Question 9

Quiz 28 Level 1

Questions

Answers

#		Question	Answer
1		What do the British call the muffler of a car?	*The silencer*
2		The archaeopteryx, which lived at the time of the dinosaurs, was a primitive type of what?	*Bird*
3		What does a botanist study?	*Plants*
4		What is geometry the study of?	*Properties of shapes, lines, and angles*
5		A giraffe has the same number of bones in its neck as a human: true or false?	*True*
6		What do ligaments connect?	*Bones*
7		What is precipitation?	*Rainfall (including frozen types)*
8		What part of a car can come in disk and drum form?	*Brakes*
9		What is the closest living relative to the mastodon, which is now extinct?	*Elephant*
10		Giant redwood trees are natives of which continent?	*North America*
11		John Logie Baird invented which means of communication?	*Television*
12		The base of the Egyptian pyramids was what shape?	*Square*
13		How many bits in a byte?	*Eight*
14		Which species has the Latin name *Homo sapiens*?	*Human beings*
15		How many teeth does an average adult have?	*32*

Quiz 27
Question 7

Quiz 27
Question 2

Quiz 29 Level 1

Questions

Answers

#		Question	Answer
1		John Glenn became the first American to do what, in 1962?	*Orbit the Earth in a spacecraft*
2		What machine first worked for a living in 1961?	*Robot*
3		What type of animal is a grebe?	*A bird*
4		What is a half plus an eighth?	*Five-eighths*
5		What is the name of the imaginary line around which a ball spins?	*The axis*
6		What sort of region could be described as being arid?	*One that is very dry, such as a desert*
7		The Swedish scientist Anders Celsius invented a method of measuring what?	*Temperature*
8		A conning tower juts up from the top of what type of vehicle?	*Submarine*
9		Fill in the symbols to complete this number sentence: 14 ? 6 ? 3 = 17.	*+ and -*
10		What kind of vehicle runs on rails on the road?	*A streetcar*
11		A mile is about 1.6 km. How many kilometers are there in 30 miles?	*About 48*
12		By which informal name is the disease BSE known?	*Mad Cow Disease*
13		Ursa Major, Libra, Casseiopia, and Virgo are names for what?	*Constellations*
14		Which organ contains the duodenum, jejunum, and ileum?	*The small intestine*
15		What everyday object has a thin coil of wire called a filament?	*A light bulb*

Quiz 30
Question 11

Quiz 30
Question 1

Quiz 30
Question 14

Quiz 30 Level 1

Questions

Answers

#	Question	Answer
1	How many legs do all insects have?	*Six*
2	If two angles of a triangle add up to 140 degrees, what must the third angle be?	*40 degrees*
3	How many teeth are there in a full set of primary ("milk") teeth?	*20*
4	Which planet has the same name as a type of metal?	*Mercury*
5	If a material is an adhesive, what does it do?	*It sticks things together*
6	Why do certain animals have webbed feet?	*To allow them to swim faster*
7	Which scientist won a Nobel prize for Chemistry for her work investigating radioactivity?	*Marie Curie*
8	How many eggs are there in six and a half dozen?	*78*
9	Which type of blood cells carry oxygen?	*Red blood cells*
10	How much of the Moon is visible during a New Moon?	*None (it is all in shadow)*
11	What is unusual about the Venus fly-trap and the pitcher plant?	*They both trap and eat insects*
12	Using only the digits 4, 5, and 1 make two even numbers.	*154 and 514*
13	What were *Skylab* and *Salyut* early examples of?	*Space station*
14	What is the albumen of an egg?	*The white*
15	Which muscle is in the back of the leg, below the knee?	*The calf*

Quiz 29
Question 15

Quiz 29
Question 10

Quiz 29
Question 13

Quiz 31 Level 1

Questions

Answers

#		Question	Answer
1		Astronomers once believed that which planet had canals on its surface?	*Mars*
2		Where would you find a flying jib?	*On a sailboat (a type of sail)*
3		What does a horticulturist study?	*The way plants can be grown*
4		What would a doctor use a sphygmomanometer to measure—height, blood pressure, or weight?	*Blood pressure*
5		Two numbers added together make 20, but multiplied together make 91. What are they?	*7 and 13*
6		Which reddish-brown metal is formed into thin wires which conduct electricity?	*Copper*
7		What are Saturn's rings made of?	*Rock fragments*
8		Who was the first person in space?	*Yuri Gagarin*
9		In 1938 what did German physicists Otto Hahn and Fritz Strassman achieve?	*They split the atom*
10		Which American animal, with a northern and crab-eating variety, has a bushy ringed tail?	*Raccoon*
11		Inches, pounds, and miles are all measurements in which system?	*Imperial*
12		What is a gale?	*A very strong wind*
13		What is the name for the body's liquid waste ?	*Urine*
14		What is 0.125 as a fraction?	*One eighth*
15		A toy car travels 30 cm with six wheel turns. How far would it go with four turns?	*20 cm*

Quiz 32
Question 12

Quiz 32
Question 10

Quiz 32
Question 2

Quiz 32 Level 1

Questions

Answers

1		What is 0.75 of 24?	*18*
2		What type of animal is a tarantula?	*Spider*
3		What type of object can be either a red giant, white dwarf, or black dwarf?	*A star*
4		Smoking tobacco harms two major organs of the body; one is the lungs, what is the other?	*The heart*
5		How many grams in a kilogram?	*1,000*
6		Which grow to be larger, African or Asian elephants?	*African*
7		What is the boiling point of water in the Celsius scale?	*100 degrees*
8		Which liquid do people put in car radiators to prevent ice from forming in the winter?	*Antifreeze*
9		What part of the body does arthritis affect?	*The bones*
10		What feature links penguins, rheas, ostriches, and kiwis?	*They are all birds that cannot fly*
11		Which English scientist developed the first modern theory about how gravity works?	*Sir Isaac Newton*
12		Where could you find a stigma, carpels, and sepals?	*In a flower*
13		How many weeks are there in five years?	*260*
14		Which planets, apart from Saturn, have rings?	*Jupiter, Uranus, and Neptune*
15		Are eggs produced by male or female plants?	*Females*

Quiz 31
Question 7

Quiz 31
Question 4

Quiz 33 Level 1

Questions

Answers

1		How many people or things are there in a quintet?	*Five*
2		With what sort of power are the engineers James Watt and Thomas Newcomen associated?	*Steam*
3		Pneumonia affects which part of the body?	*The lungs*
4		Why is an elephant's footprint no deeper than a human's?	*Because its huge foot spreads the weight*
5		Is black ice really black?	*No—it is clear*
6		What sort of scientist would be concerned with isobars, high pressure fronts, and occluded fronts?	*Meteorologist*
7		Which is the odd one out: whale, shark, cod, skate?	*Whale (the others are all fish)*
8		What is the total number of spots on a six-sided die?	*21*
9		Which object, used to make things look bigger, can make paper burn?	*A magnifying glass*
10		Which objects in space have tails up to 100 million km long?	*Comets*
11		John Loudon McAdam invented a system for strengthening the surface of what?	*Roads*
12		Iron will only rust if both air and what else are present?	*Water*
13		Who has more bones—a man or a woman?	*They have the same number*
14		Did the United States, China, or the USSR send the first satellite into space?	*USSR*
15		Combustion is the scientific word for which process?	*Burning*

Quiz 34
Question 8

Quiz 34
Question 7

Quiz 34
Question 3

Quiz 34 Level 1

Questions

Answers

		Questions	Answers
1		What do these have in common: Appalachians, Dolomites, Urals, and Atlas?	*They are all mountain ranges*
2		What is one fifth of one fifth?	*One twenty-fifth*
3		What was *Voyager II*?	*A space probe*
4		What type of person would have to study anatomy and physiology?	*A doctor or surgeon*
5		Which bones form a cage around your lungs?	*The ribs*
6		How far is the Sun from the Earth?	*93 million miles (150 million km)*
7		What do the British call a flashlight?	*A torch*
8		How many arms does a starfish have?	*Five*
9		What does the prefix "iso" mean in the words isosceles and isobar?	*The same*
10		George Stephenson invented what form of transportation?	*The steam locomotive*
11		What was the name of the first man on the Moon?	*Neil Armstrong*
12		If a doctor gave you an antihistamine, how would you be affected?	*Your nose would become less stuffy*
13		Who invented the first car driven by an internal combustion engine?	*Karl Benz*
14		What is the main ingredient of paper?	*Wood pulp*
15		If you divided a rectangle diagonally, what two shapes would you create?	*Two triangles*

Quiz 33
Question 9

Quiz 33
Question 10

Quiz 35 Level 1

Questions

Answers

		Question	Answer
1		What word describes the horizontal and vertical lines on a graph?	*Axis*
2		If it is 2 p.m. in London, what time is it in New York?	*9 a.m.*
3		What is classified by the letters, A, B, AB, and O?	*Blood types*
4		What kind of airplane was a Lancaster? Quiz 36 Question 13	*A bomber*
5		If you are looking forward on a ship, which way is starboard?	*To the right*
6		How many millimeters are there in a centimeter?	*Ten*
7		Why do reptiles bask in the sunshine?	*To warm their blood*
8		Alfred Nobel, who founded the Peace Prizes, invented what in 1866?	*Dynamite*
9		What is a fjord?	*A narrow, steep-sided inlet*
10		In which sport would a "bobber" be used to indicate a bite?	*Fishing*
11		What word describes a solid shape with circles at each end?	*Cylinder*
12		In which year did Yuri Gagarin make the first manned space flight: 1959, 1961, or 1963?	*1961*
13		What sort of patient would a pediatrician treat?	*Children*
14		What type of animal are vipers, adders, and mambos?	*Snakes*
15		What is the normal body temperature of a healthy person?	*98.6°F (37°C)*

Quiz 36
Question 5

Quiz 36 Level 1

Questions

Answers

#		Question	Answer
1		Where would you find the rudder of an airplane?	*On the tail fin*
2		What material was used to produce LP records?	*Vinyl*
3	$\sqrt{x}$	How many hours are there in five days?	*120*
4		On which continent is Angel Falls, the world's highest waterfall?	*South America*
5		What part of a fish aids buoyancy?	*Swimbladder*
6		What blood problem affects someone with hemophilia?	*The blood does not clot properly*
7		A fuel cell is a type of what?	*Battery*
8		What happens when pottery is "fired"?	*It is baked until it becomes hard*
9		Euclid, the Greek mathematician, is known as the father of what?	*Geometry*
10	$\sqrt{x}$	How many grams are there in 5 kg?	*5,000*
11		What is smog?	*A mixture of smoke and fog*
12		Which South American animal hangs from trees and seems to spend its whole life sleeping?	*The giant sloth*
13		What would a serial or parallel cable be used for?	*Connecting devices to a computer*
14		Which type of scientist would study quasars, pulsars, and asteroids?	*An astronomer*
15		You would find a cuticle at the base of what parts of the body?	*Fingernails and toenails*

Quiz 35
Question 10

Quiz 35
Question 4

Quiz 37 Level 2

Questions

Answers

1		Is it true that water expands (grows bigger) as it freezes?	*Yes*
2		Which age followed the Stone Age?	*The Bronze Age*
3		Which religion celebrates Hanukkah for eight days each December?	*The Jewish religion*
4		Where would you find a ligament?	*In a joint*
5		How long is the term of a US Representative?	*Two years*
6		Which western European nation has the largest population?	*Germany (about 80 million people)*
7		Which river flows through Vienna?	*The Danube*
8		Who died in St. Helena?	*Napoleon in 1821*
9		One third is approximately which decimal fraction?	*0.333*
10		Through which organs do whales breathe?	*Lungs*
11		Which insect has larvae called daphnia?	*Dragonfly*
12		Which armored fighting vehicle runs on tracks?	*The tank*
13		Who did Dr. Jekyll change into?	*Edward Hyde*
14		What is the Irish name for Ireland?	*Eire*
15		What is the name of the spear that is thrown in track and field events?	*Javelin*

Quiz 38
Question 12

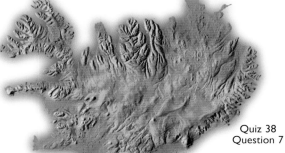

Quiz 38
Question 7

Quiz 38
Question 2

Quiz 38 Level 2

Questions

Answers

#	Question	Answer
1	What is the name for the large flat teeth at the back of the mouth used for grinding food?	*The molars*
2	His thoughts were published in a little red book. Who was he?	*Chairman Mao*
3	There are two kinds of electric current. One is direct current, or DC; what is the other?	*Alternating current or AC*
4	How old is the Earth — 3 billion, 3.5 billion, 4 billion, or 4.5 billion years?	*About 4.5 billion years old*
5	What is the currency of Greece?	*The drachma*
6	Which domestic animal is sacred to the Hindus?	*The cow*
7	Reykjavik is the capital of which country?	*Iceland*
8	What is the universe?	*All of space and everything in it*
9	What is a male pig called?	*A boar*
10	Where was the Battle of Bunker Hill fought?	*Boston (in the Revolutionary War)*
11	Who was *Australopithecus*?	*A form of ancient man*
12	How many eyes did the Cyclops have?	*One*
13	Which class of creatures contains more than two-thirds of all known species?	*Insects*
14	Frogs can breathe air through their skins. True or false?	*True*
15	What is the opposite of *loyalty*?	*Disloyalty*

Quiz 37
Question 13

Quiz 37
Question 12

Quiz 37
Question 11

Quiz 39 Level 2

Questions

Answers

#	Question	Answer
1	What color are pistachio nuts?	Green
2	What do you call people who have no permanent home and move around in search of pasture?	Nomads
3	Which country is made up of two main islands, North Island and South Island?	New Zealand
4	What is an air-breathing gastropod mollusk, with a spiral shell, better known as?	A snail
5	What is a toga?	A type of cloak worn in ancient Rome
6	What are your canine teeth?	The pointed teeth, or eye teeth
7	How many sides are there in a quadrilateral?	4 sides
8	Where does the Sun set?	In the west
9	What are chickens, ducks, geese, partridges, and pheasants?	They are all poultry
10	What word means *to put off until another time*?	Postpone
11	What collapsed in the Wall Street Crash?	The U.S. stock market
12	What are conduction, convection, and radiation?	They are three ways in which heat travels
13	Of which country is Colonel Qaddafi the head?	Libya
14	Who became President after John F. Kennedy was assassinated?	Lyndon B. Johnson
15	The height of a mountain is measured from what base?	Sea level

Quiz 40
Question 2

Quiz 40 Level 2

Questions

Answers

#		Question	Answer
1		What causes the common cold?	*Viruses*
2		What were the pyramids in ancient Egypt used for?	*Royal tombs*
3		To what group of animals do rats belong?	*Rodents*
4		Which sport do we associate with Steffi Graf?	*Tennis*
5		What is another name for Northern Ireland?	*Ulster*
6		What is a part of the circumference of a circle called?	*An arc*
7		J.M.W. Turner was what?	*An English painter*
8		What is the spiral part of a screw called?	*The thread*
9		Which soft-bodied sea creature looks like a flower?	*The sea anemone*
10		St. Petersburg was renamed Leningrad. What is it called now?	*St. Petersburg*
11		How many lives are cats said to have?	*9*
12		From which plant is linen made?	*Flax*
13		What destroyed Nagasaki in World War II?	*An atom bomb*
14		Who wrote the words to "The Star Spangled Banner"?	*Francis Scott Key*
15		Who were Virgil, Horace, and Ovid?	*Roman poets*

Quiz 39
Question 3

Quiz 39
Question 4

Quiz 41 Level 2

Answers

#	Question	Answer
1	Who composed the ballets *Swan Lake*, *The Nutcracker,* and *The Sleeping Beauty*?	*Tchaikovsky*
2	What is a fandango?	*A Spanish dance*
3	Where are the Solomon Islands?	*In the Pacific Ocean*
4	Ginger, cloves, pepper, and nutmeg are all what?	*Spices*
5	Alfred Nobel, who donated the Nobel Prizes, made his fortune from what?	*Explosives*
6	How do the British spell *color*?	*Colour*
7	Where could you look for starfish, lugworms, razor shells, and cockles?	*On sandy or muddy beaches*
8	Who wrote about the *Cat in the Hat*?	*Dr. Seuss*
9	A dogfish is a small what?	*A small shark*
10	Which of the following countries are monarchies: Denmark, Norway, Sweden?	*All of them*
11	What are bakelite and celluloid?	*Early plastics*
12	Which is the only French-speaking province of Canada?	*Quebec*
13	What are the chances of throwing two heads if you toss a coin twice?	*1 in 4*
14	What does Saturday's child do?	*Works hard for a living*
15	What is seven-eighths of 56?	*49*

Quiz 42
Question 5

Quiz 42
Question 11

Quiz 42 Level 2

Answers

#		Question	Answer
1		Which science deals with heat, light, sound, electricity, and mechanics?	*Physics*
2		What musical instrument developed from virginals and harpsichords?	*The piano*
3		Name an animal eaten for meat, whose fat, skin, and hair give lard, leather, and brushes?	*The pig*
4		How many notes are there in an octave?	*8*
5		Which Australian animal is a mammal that lays eggs but feeds its young on its milk?	*The platypus*
6		Which country do the Azores and Madeira islands belong to?	*Portugal*
7		What substance is used to make cups, saucers, tiles, and bricks?	*Pottery*
8		In grammar, what kind of words are *he*, *she*, *it*, *they*?	*Pronouns*
9		What is the name for a star that gives out regular pulses of radio waves?	*A pulsar*
10		Which disease is spread by the bite of infected dogs or wild animals?	*Rabies*
11		Which English sailor, soldier and explorer took tobacco to Europe from North America?	*Sir Walter Raleigh*
12		Which sea separates northeast Africa from Arabia?	*The Red Sea*
13		What striped animal gave its name to a British pedestrian crossing?	*The zebra*
14		Which long river rises in Switzerland and flows through Germany to Holland and the North Sea?	*The Rhine*
15		Complete the phrase: *as fresh as a ....*	*Daisy*

Quiz 41
Question 4

Quiz 41
Question 9

Quiz 43 Level 2

#	Question	Answer
1	Who was Paul Cézanne?	*A famous French painter*
2	Which country produces the most gold?	*South Africa*
3	What is a mural?	*A painting on a wall*
4	What do daffodils, bluebells, and crocuses have in common?	*They all grow from bulbs*
5	Methane is the main part of which widely used fuel?	*Natural gas*
6	What is eaten with cream at the Wimbledon tennis matches?	*Strawberries*
7	What is the capital of Kenya?	*Nairobi*
8	Who was Mowgli?	*The boy in* Jungle Book
9	On which Japanese city was the first atomic bomb dropped?	*Hiroshima*
10	How many periods are there in an ice hockey game?	*Three*
11	Who wrote *Mein Kampf*?	*Adolf Hitler*
12	Which of these two, coal and oil, is a fossil fuel?	*They both are fossil fuels*
13	Which Australian state is an island?	*Tasmania*
14	What is a terrapin?	*A freshwater turtle*
15	What is a substance called that gives off heat when it burns?	*A fuel*

Quiz 44
Question 2

Quiz 44
Question 14

Quiz 44
Question 11

Quiz 44 Level 2

1		When does Lent end?	*On Easter Sunday*
2		Which insect makes its nest from chewed-up mud or wood?	*The wasp*
3		The Adriatic and Aegean seas are part of which sea?	*The Mediterranean*
4		Which organs remove waste products from the blood?	*The kidneys*
5		Seoul is the capital of which Korea?	*South Korea*
6		What is the masculine of mare?	*Stallion*
7		What is another name for ground nuts?	*Peanuts*
8		Which singer was known as *The King*?	*Elvis Presley*
9		Which English scientist put forward the law of gravity?	*Sir Isaac Newton*
10		From which tree do we get syrup?	*The sugar maple*
11		Which is the savage fish from South America that attacks the flesh of other fish and mammals?	*The piranha*
12		Which black birds live in the Tower of London?	*Ravens*
13		Which vitamin are oranges full of?	*Vitamin C*
14		What is the name for the fibrous tissue which joins a muscle to a bone?	*A tendon*
15		What does *frivolous* mean?	*Silly, not useful*

Quiz 43
Question 14

Quiz 43
Question 11

Quiz 45 Level 2

1	In which country is the Tigris River?	Iraq
2	Who had a magic lamp?	Aladdin
3	What is a migraine?	A severe, prolonged headache
4	What is silent acting called?	Mime
5	The Missouri is a tributary of which river?	The Mississippi
6	The United States fought a war against which country in 1898?	Spain
7	Which American spacecraft made its first flight in 1981?	The Shuttle
8	What is the capital of Pakistan?	Islamabad
9	What is the name of an automatic device for controlling temperature?	A thermostat
10	What high office did George Mondale, Spiro Agnew, and Dan Quayle hold?	U.S. vice president
11	What is another name for a puma?	A cougar
12	Where is the U.S. Naval Academy located?	Annapolis, Maryland
13	Which prehistoric catlike animal had two canine teeth about 8 inches long?	The saber-toothed tiger
14	Which warrior caste of Japan followed a strict code of behavior?	The Samurai
15	What does it mean to be *cut to the quick*? Quiz 46 Question 13	To be deeply hurt

Quiz 46 Level 2

1		Who started cubism and is considered the most famous modern painter?	*Pablo Picasso*
2		What was another name for the Plague?	*The Black Death*
3		Which nutritional substances are milk, meat, eggs, fish, and nuts rich in?	*Protein*
4		The Red Sea is a part of which ocean?	*The Indian Ocean*
5		What is the capital of Romania?	*Bucharest*
6		What happens if iron and steel are left exposed to air and moisture?	*They rust*
7		Which city in Nevada is famous for gambling?	*Las Vegas*
8		Who wrote *Treasure Island*?	*Robert Louis Stevenson*
9		Which sea mammal looks like a seal but has fur on its body and, unlike the seal, has ears?	*The sea lion*
10		What is the opposite of *legal*?	*Illegal*
11		Which worldwide disease has been wiped out by vaccination?	*Smallpox*
12		General Franco was dictator of which country?	*Spain*
13		The Cavaliers and Roundheads were opponents in which war?	*The English Civil War*
14		Which country's flag shows a red maple leaf?	*Canada*
15		What is a joey?	*A newborn kangaroo*

Quiz 45
Question 7

Quiz 47 Level 2

1	What kind of flag is waved to show the winner of an automobile race?	*A black and white checkered flag*
2	Which state is called the *Lone Star State*?	*Texas*
3	Who wrote the *Just So Stories*?	*Rudyard Kipling*
4	In swimming pools, which chemical is added to water to kill germs?	*Chlorine*
5	Who was President when the United States entered World War II in 1941?	*Franklin D. Roosevelt*
6	Which vegetable makes you cry?	*The onion*
7	What is the name for a substance that makes a person immune to a certain disease?	*A vaccine*
8	Where is Ecuador?	*In northwestern South America*
9	What does *making a mountain out of a molehill* mean?	*Exaggerating a problem*
10	Who was the first American President to be assassinated?	*Abraham Lincoln*
11	Which South American animal is used as a pack horse by the people of the Andes?	*The llama*
12	Which river do Hindus consider sacred?	*The Ganges*
13	What is an expert judge, especially of food and drink, called?	*A connoisseur*
14	What do you call a male goose?	*A gander*
15	Which instrument did Chopin play?	*The piano*

Quiz 48
Question 9

Quiz 48
Question 15

Quiz 48 Level 2

1		Lhasa is the capital of which country?	*Tibet*
2		Who flew the *Spirit of St. Louis* across the Atlantic?	*Charles Lindbergh*
3		Which sea did Moses cross with the Israelites?	*The Red Sea*
4		A gun that fires a bullet along a spirally grooved barrel is called...?	*A rifle*
5		What is the name of the largest planet in the Solar System?	*Jupiter*
6		Who was the Soviet communist leader during World War II?	*Joseph Stalin*
7		Who is the messenger of love in Roman myths?	*Cupid, with his bow and arrow*
8		Of which family was Bonnie Prince Charlie?	*The Stuarts*
9		Who was the mythological figure with a human head and lion's body?	*The sphinx*
10		Mars was the Roman god of what?	*War*
11		What is the weak mixture of acetic acid and water, used for flavoring food and for pickling?	*Vinegar*
12		Which is the most commonly used letter in the English alphabet?	*The letter E*
13		The name of which animal means *a thousand legs*?	*The millipede*
14		What is the opposite of *obedient*?	*Disobedient*
15		How many legs does a crab have?	*10*

Quiz 47
Question 3

Quiz 47
Question 6

Quiz 49 Level 2

Questions

Answers

		Question	Answer
1		What did Thomas Chippendale make?	*Furniture*
2		Was the battle of Lepanto in 1471 fought at sea or on land?	*At sea*
3		Against which disease did Edward Jenner pioneer vaccination in 1796?	*Smallpox*
4		Which U.S. president resigned over the Watergate affair?	*Richard Nixon*
5		Who wrote "The Road Not Taken"?	*Robert Frost*
6		Whose army are the Russians fighting in Tolstoy's novel *War and Peace?*	*The French army of Napoleon*
7		What year was the Persian Gulf War—1980, 1985, or 1991?	*1991*
8		What was the name of the first genetically cloned mammal, a sheep?	*Dolly*
9		What is the first name of Queen Elizabeth II's sister?	*Margaret*
10		Which city opened a huge Millennium Dome in 2000?	*London*
11		Which country had a "Glorious Revolution" in 1688?	*England*
12		From which countries did the Vikings begin their raids around northern Europe?	*Sweden, Norway, Finland, Denmark*
13		Which three weapons were first used during World War I (1914-1918)?	*Airplanes, tanks, and submarines*
14		Who started building the Tower of London in 1078?	*William the Conqueror*
15		Which English poet wrote a famous poem about daffodils?	*William Wordsworth*

Quiz 50
Question 3

Quiz 50 Level 2

Questions

Answers

		Questions	Answers
1		In which century were machine guns invented?	*19th century*
2		In the 1800s Joseph Henry and Michael Faraday separately made a discovery about magnets: what?	*That a magnet has an electrical effect*
3		In a medieval motte and bailey castle, was the motte a mound or a ditch?	*A mound*
4		In which century were the first aerial bombs used?	*19th century, hung from Austrian balloons*
5		What was a "nilometer" used for in ancient Egypt?	*To measure the depth of the River Nile*
6		What is the name of the hill near Jerusalem where Jesus was crucified?	*Calvary*
7		Who wrote *Gulliver's Travels*?	*Jonathan Swift*
8		Which British prime minister was born in Edinburgh in 1953?	*Tony Blair*
9		What killed the Greek playwright Aeschylus?	*A stone dropped by an eagle*
10		What was the favorite weapon of the Mongols?	*Bow and arrow*
11		Who ruled the Soviet Union from 1924 to 1953?	*Stalin*
12		Carib Indians thought Spanish explorers wore tortoise shells: what were the shells?	*Steel armor breastplates*
13		Who was the first Roman emperor to become a Christian?	*Constantine*
14		Who wrote the novel *For Whom the Bell Tolls*?	*Ernest Hemingway*
15		Which scientist discovered oxygen?	*Joseph Priestley*

Quiz 49
Question 1

Quiz 49
Question 12

Quiz 51 Level 2

Questions

Answers

#	Question	Answer
1	Which country was led by a man who called himself Marshal Tito?	*Yugoslavia*
2	What was the Pyroscaphe of 1783?	*The first steam-driven boat*
3	In which year was the integrated circuit invented: 1959, 1969, or 1979?	*1959*
4	Idi Amin expelled 40,000 British Asians from which country?	*Uganda*
5	Which English king is known as "the Unready"?	*Ethelred*
6	Which U.S. president was assassinated in 1901?	*William McKinley*
7	From which Celtic tribe did Boudicca come?	*The Iceni*
8	Which English king led his army to victory at Agincourt?	*Henry V*
9	What Chinese invention of about 1400BC revolutionized the making of clay pots?	*The potter's wheel*
10	On which mountain is Noah's Ark believed to have come to rest?	*Mount Ararat, in modern Turkey*
11	What transportation device did William Henson dream up in 1843?	*An aerial steam carriage but it never flew*
12	Did a concentric castle have one wall or more than one?	*More than one*
13	What was the first supersonic airliner, which entered service in 1976?	*Concorde*
14	Which ancient people discovered the principle of perspective in art?	*The Romans*
15	Which giant birds once roamed New Zealand?	*Moas*

Quiz 52
Question 3

Quiz 52
Question 5

Quiz 52
Question 15

Quiz 52 Level 2

Questions

Answers

1	What record did the Bell X-1 set in 1947?	*First supersonic flight by a piloted aircraft*
2	In which country was the war of the Three Henrys fought?	*France, in 1585*
3	What was one of the main finds at the Sutton Hoo burial ground?	*An ancient battle helmet*
4	What year did the Berlin Wall come down?	*1989*
5	On which planet did the *Viking 1* probe land in 1976?	*Mars*
6	Who wrote the first draft of the U.S. Constitution: Jefferson, Lincoln, or Grant?	*Jefferson*
7	Which early central American people built pyramids and invented a calendar?	*The Maya*
8	Who was the first man to fly at Mach 1, the speed of sound at sea level?	*Charles Yeager*
9	In which century did soldiers start wearing grey or khaki uniforms?	*19th century*
10	Which great Islamic monument was built in Jerusalem in AD691?	*The Dome of the Rock*
11	Which beautiful woman was stolen from her husband and caused the Trojan war?	*Helen of Troy*
12	Which country's army was led by Gustavus Adolphus in the 1600s?	*Sweden*
13	Where did *Columbia* go in 1981?	*Into space; it was the first U.S. space shuttle*
14	What form of propulsion did Frank Whittle pioneer?	*Jet propulsion*
15	How did France's Queen Marie Antoinette die?	*She was executed by guillotine*

Quiz 51
Question 8

Quiz 51
Question 7

Quiz 53 Level 2

Questions

Answers

#	Question	Answer
1	What was President Lincoln doing when he was shot in 1865?	*Watching a play*
2	What was the name of the rocket that sent the Apollo spacecraft to the Moon?	**Saturn 5**
3	Which bloodthirsty Roman emperor was nicknamed "Little Boots"?	*Caligula*
4	Who was the Norse god of thunder?	*Thor*
5	How many perfect numbers are known: 2, 12, 100, 1000?	*12*
6	Which 1950s singer sang with *The Crickets*?	***Buddy Holly***
7	What did Alexander Graham Bell invent in 1876?	*The telephone*
8	What does the word "dinosaur" actually mean? Quiz 54 Question 3	*It is Greek for "terrible lizard"*
9	What was the family name of Diana, Princess of Wales?	*Spencer*
10	In which 18th-century war did Prussia fight France, Austria, and Russia?	*Seven Years' War*
11	What happened to the American passenger pigeon early in the 20th century?	*It became extinct*
12	In which year did the prophet Muhammad flee from Mecca to Medina?	*622*
13	Was the *Turbinia* of 1897 a steam-turbine ship or a kind of airship?	*A steam-turbine ship*
14	Which country was ruled by the Shang dynasty?	*China*
15	When was the first hovercraft built: 1939, 1949, or 1959?	*1959* Quiz 54 Question 10

Quiz 54 Level 2

Questions

Answers

#		Question	Answer
1		Which country set up the first national park?	*The USA (Yellowstone, 1872)*
2		In which city were the Beatles born?	*Liverpool*
3		Who commanded the Confederate forces in the U.S. Civil War?	*General Robert E. Lee*
4		After whom is the orbital Space Telescope named?	*Edwin Hubble*
5		In which war was the Battle of Bull Run?	*US Civil War*
6		Which big cat lives in the cold mountains of Asia?	*The snow leopard*
7		Who was the patron goddess of Athens?	*Athene*
8		Who was it that gave a speech beginning "I have a dream"?	*Martin Luther King*
9		In which decade were talking films introduced?	*The 1920s*
10		Which war was fought between 1950 and 1953?	*The Korean War*
11		Which countries were joined politically in 1707?	*England and Scotland*
12		Which Shakespeare play is about a Scottish king's murder?	**Macbeth**
13		In which country were cars first mass-produced in factories?	*United States*
14		What, in ancient Greece, was an amphora?	*A two-handled storage jar*
15		In what year did Fleming discover penicillin?	*1928*

Quiz 53
Question 14

Quiz 53
Question 7

Quiz 53
Question 8

Quiz 55 Level 2

Questions

Answers

		Questions	Answers
1		When did nuclear power plants start to generate electricity: 1930s or 1950s?	*1950s*
2		When was the first revolver made?	*1835*
3		What was different about sending a letter after 1840?	*Postage stamps were used for the first time*
4		Who was Ned Kelly?	*An Australian outlaw in the 1800s*
5		What were the small, hairy creatures that were the heroes in *The Lord of the Rings*?	*Hobbits*
6		In what year did William Shakespeare die: 1606, 1616, or 1626?	*1616*
7		Which human body part was the first to be successfully transplanted in 1954?	*The kidney*
8		In which century did people first use handkerchiefs?	*The 16th century*
9		Which Swedish tennis player won 5 Wimbledon men's singles titles in a row (1976 to 1980)?	*Bjorn Borg*
10		What were the *Merrimack* and *Monitor*?	*The first armored ships to fight*
11		What did Alice go through to get to Wonderland?	*A rabbit's burrow*
12		Which construction, the first to be built entirely of iron, was made in Coalbrookdale, England?	*An iron bridge*
13		Which president ordered the dropping of the first atomic bomb on Japan?	*Harry S. Truman*
14		For which baseball team did Lou Gehrig play?	*The New York Yankees*
15		Which decade of the 20th century was known as The Jazz Age?	*The 1920s*

Quiz 56
Question 1

Quiz 56 Level 2

Questions

Answers

#	Question	Answer
1	What do we call the jagged tops of castle walls, through which archers could fire?	*Crenellations*
2	Which part of China passed from British rule in 1997?	*Hong Kong*
3	What did a man named Gatling invent in 1863?	*A rapid-firing gun (the first machine gun)*
4	How did Sir John Franklin meet his death in 1847?	*He and his men were trapped in Arctic ice*
5	What subjects were early Islamic artists forbidden to paint?	*Animals and plants*
6	What kind of weapon was a Lee Enfield?	*A rifle*
7	What is the first book in the Bible?	*Genesis*
8	Which famous ship, which sank in 1912 on its first voyage, featured in a blockbuster movie?	*The* Titanic
9	Which natural wonder did Cook explore off eastern Australia?	*The Great Barrier Reef*
10	Which great Roman leader and general wrote an account of his campaigns in Gaul?	*Julius Caesar*
11	What did the steamship *Savannah* cross in 1819?	*The Atlantic Ocean*
12	In what language was the poem *Beowulf* written?	*Anglo-Saxon (or old English)*
13	Which Spanish soldier conquered the Incas in the 16th century?	*Francisco Pizarro*
14	Which sea route did Amundsen navigate in 1903-1906?	*The North-West Passage*
15	Which land was explored by the Viking Erik the Red in about 982?	*Greenland*

Quiz 55
Question 4

Quiz 55
Question 12

Quiz 57 Level 2

Questions

Answers

		Questions	Answers
1		Where was the world's biggest expanse of prairie?	North America (before 1900)
2		Which Egyptian queen was the lover of the Roman Mark Antony?	Cleopatra
3		In which country was the 1916 Easter Rising?	Ireland
4		Where was the battle of Dien Bien Phu fought in 1954?	Vietnam
5		What strong but delicate kind of ceramic was invented in China in about AD700?	Porcelain
6		Settlers in the Wild West tamed mustangs: what were mustangs?	Wild horses
7		What do we call poetry that is memorized and recited but not written down?	Oral poetry
8		Manet and Monet were both famous French . . . what?	Painters
9		What was the first name of the Mongol leader Khan, grandfather of Kublai Khan?	Genghis
10		What was the date of the D-Day invasion during World War II?	June 6, 1944
11		What was a prairie schooner?	A covered wagon used by Western pioneers
12		Who was vice president under Jimmy Carter?	Walter Mondale
13		Which American poet wrote *Leaves of Grass*?	Walt Whitman
14		Who commanded television's first starship *Enterprise*?	Captain James Kirk
15		Which two Russian cities endured long sieges during World War II?	Leningrad and Stalingrad

Quiz 58
Question 12

Quiz 58
Question 15

Quiz 58 Level 2

Questions

Answers

#	Question	Answer
1	Who invented the lightning conductor in June 1752?	*Benjamin Franklin*
2	From which country did Admiral Cheng Ho lead voyages of discovery?	*China*
3	Which river features in the title of a famous waltz tune by Strauss?	*The Danube (The Blue Danube)*
4	Which invader won a battle at Panipat in India in 1526?	*Babur*
5	Which great African empire was founded in about AD750?	*Ghana*
6	Luther Burbank was born in America in 1849: did he grow plants, fight battles, or write songs?	*He grew (and studied) plants*
7	Who first believed that the Earth was round: the ancient Greeks, the Vikings, or Columbus?	*The ancient Greeks*
8	Which ancient city did the archeologist Heinrich Schliemann dig for?	*Troy*
9	By what name is Siddhartha Gautama better-known?	*Buddha*
10	Hosni Mubarak became president of which African country in 1981?	*Egypt*
11	Which country did Konrad Adenauer lead from 1949 to 1963?	*West Germany*
12	The ancient cities of Mohenjo Daro and Harappa were in which country?	*India*
13	A Roman city buried by a volcano in AD79 was rediscovered in the 1700s: what was its name?	*Pompeii*
14	What job did John Adams take on in 1796?	*President of the United States*
15	What was a bombard, invented in about 1340?	*An early cannon*

Quiz 57
Question 11

Quiz 59 Level 2

Questions

Answers

#		Question	Answer
1		In *Peter Pan*, what is the name of the villainous pirate captain?	*Captain Hook*
2		What were searchlights used for in World War II?	*To pick out enemy bombers at night*
3		Which French female soldier was burned to death in 1431 by the English?	*Joan of Arc*
4		Who was the most famous British scientist of the Middle Ages?	*Roger Bacon (about 1220-1292)*
5		Who succeeded Harry Truman as president in 1953?	*Dwight Eisenhower*
6		On which Pacific islands, visited by Darwin between 1831 and 1836, do giant tortoises live?	*The Galapagos*
7		Which record was broken by Donald Campbell in the *Bluebird* on September 19, 1956?	*The water speed record (286 mph)*
8		What did the ancient Greeks call the Straits of Gibraltar, leading to the Atlantic?	*The Pillars of Hercules*
9		In which continent was Ernest Shackleton an explorer?	*Antarctica*
10		Who wrote "Rip Van Winkle"?	*Washington Irving*
11		In which war was the battle of Naseby?	*English Civil War*
12		What was cuneiform?	*The earliest kind of writing*
13		What did John Bardeen, William Shockley, and Walter Brattain invent in the 1940s?	*The integrated circuit, or microchip*
14		Which poet recited his work at president Kennedy's inauguration in 1961?	*Robert Frost*
15		Which European country invaded Abyssinia (Ethiopia) in the 1930s?	*Italy*

Quiz 60
Question 9

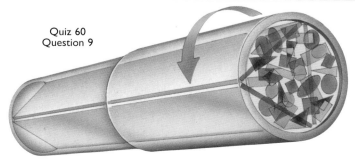

Quiz 60 Level 2

Questions   ## Answers

#	Question	Answer
1	Was Elvis Presley the singer's real name?	*Yes*
2	Who wrote *Pilgrim's Progress*?	***John Bunyan***
3	Which queen was the subject of a film called *Mrs Brown*?	***Queen Victoria***
4	Which comet did the *Giotto* space probe whizz past in 1986?	***Halley's Comet***
5	Who painted *The Laughing Cavalier*?	***Frans Hals***
6	Nineveh and Assur were the chief cities of which empire?	***Assyrian***
7	The Silk Road ran between Europe and which country?	***China***
8	On which Mediterranean island did the mythical monster the Minotaur live?	***Crete***
9	What optical toy was invented by the Scottish scientist Sir David Brewster?	***The kaleidoscope***
10	Who said, "I shall return" in World War II?	***General Douglas MacArthur***
11	What was Enrico Caruso's claim to fame: singing, motor racing, or soccer?	***Singing***
12	What flew around the world in 1957?	**Sputnik 1**, *the first artificial satellite*
13	Who led the British to victory at Quebec in 1759?	*Wolfe*
14	What country produced the writers W.B. Yeats and Sean O'Casey?	*Ireland*
15	When was Bakelite, the first artificial plastic, invented: 1879, 1909, or 1939?	*1909*

Quiz 59
Question 3

Quiz 59
Question 7

Quiz 61 Level 2

Questions

Answers

		Questions	Answers
1		Which fireproof building material can damage the lungs if breathed in?	*Asbestos*
2		A ship's crow's nest is located at the top of what?	*The main mast*
3		What is the more common term for an integer?	*A whole number*
4		How many moons does Uranus have: 6, 5, or 4?	*5*
5		What famous table did Russian, Dmitri Mendelev, produce?	*The periodic table of elements*
6		Where in your body would you find your adenoids?	*At the back of the nose and throat*
7		How many inches are there in 5 feet?	*60*
8		What vehicle was first built in 1936 by Ferdinand Porsche in Germany?	*The Volkswagen Beetle car*
9		Which has most calories: margarine or butter?	*They have about the same*
10		What device is used to listen inside the body?	*A stethoscope*
11		Which scientist of the 1800s is linked with the Theory of Evolution?	*Charles Darwin*
12		If it is spring in Canada, what season is it in New Zealand?	*Autumn*
13		On which continent would you find orangutans?	*Asia*
14		What are both the Julian and Gregorian?	*Types of calendar*
15		Which part of the body is affected by eczema?	*The skin*

Quiz 62
Question 10

Quiz 62
Question 7

Quiz 62 Level 2

Questions

Answers

		Questions	Answers
1		What does a light year measure?	*Distance (traveled by light in a year)*
2		What do you call a rock or mineral from which a metal can be extracted?	*An ore*
3		What is the soft inner part of the bone, where blood cells are made?	*The marrow*
4		If I have 14 candies and give 3 to one friend and 2 to another, how many candies do I have left?	*9*
5		If an engineer is measuring the gradient of a hillside, what is he or she finding?	*How steep it is*
6		What type of behavior is typical of most people suffering from anorexia?	*They only eat tiny amounts of food*
7		What is a boa constrictor?	*A type of snake*
8		What is a gorge?	*A narrow, steep-sided valley*
9		What sort of vehicle would a scientist at Cape Canaveral, Florida, be working on?	*A rocket*
10		What kind of weapons are Berettas?	*Guns*
11		How fast is the Earth orbiting the Sun to the nearest 5,000 mph?	*66,500 mph*
12		What insect shares its name with a swimming stroke?	*A butterfly*
13		What does the prefix "milli" mean in metric measurements?	*One-thousandth*
14		What process causes water droplets to form on a cold window?	*Condensation*
15		The science of the study of the body and its parts is called what?	*Anatomy*

Quiz 61
Question 10

Quiz 61
Question 2

Quiz 63 Level 2

Questions

Answers

#		Question	Answer
1		What type of tough string is pulled between the teeth to clean them and to strengthen the gums?	*Dental floss*
2		Which planet is known as the red planet?	*Mars*
3		What does a nutritionist specialize in?	*Food and diet*
4		What does a microscope do?	*Magnifies small objects*
5		Which part of the eye becomes wider or narrower, depending on how bright the light is?	*The pupil*
6		Acoustics is the study of what?	*Sound, and how it travels*
7		In Roman numerals, what is CLVI divided by XIII?	*XII*
8		Which kitchen utensil shares its name with a quick, light movement?	*A whisk*
9		What does it mean if an animal is a vertebrate?	*It has a backbone*
10		Which is the body's largest joint?	*The knee*
11		What is the nearest whole number to pi, which is used to measure circles?	*3 (3.14159)*
12		What was the Black Death, which killed millions of people during the Middle Ages?	*Bubonic plague, a deadly disease*
13		Where would you find an estuary?	*At the mouth of a river*
14		In which year did human beings first set foot on the Moon?	*1969*
15		Where would you find a femur bone?	*In your leg*

Quiz 64
Question 4

Quiz 64
Question 1

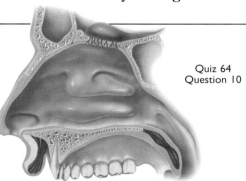

Quiz 64
Question 10

Quiz 64 Level 2

Questions

Answers

		Questions	Answers
1		What is the name for an L-shaped hexagonal rod used to undo a certain type of screw?	*An Allen key*
2		How does eating fiber help the body?	*It helps the body get rid of wastes*
3	$\sqrt{x}$	What do 25, 16, and 9 have in common?	*They are all square numbers*
4		What shape is a sphere?	*Round, like a ball*
5		What term describes trees that have cones?	*Coniferous*
6		Which animals travel in packs?	*Wolves*
7	$\sqrt{x}$	What is two thirds of two thirds?	*Four ninths*
8		What part of your body would an optometrist study?	*Your eyes*
9		What is a monocle?	*A lens worn in one eye*
10		What part of the body does nasal refer to?	*The nose*
11		The name of which type of animal means "terrible lizard" in Greek?	*Dinosaur*
12	$\sqrt{x}$	What is 75% of 444?	*333*
13		Why should people trying to lose weight remove the skin from chicken?	*Because the skin contains the most fat*
14		What is "flu" short for?	*Influenza*
15		Can bears climb trees?	*Yes*

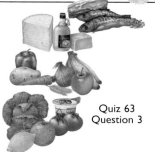

Quiz 63
Question 3

Quiz 63
Question 8

Quiz 65 Level 2

Questions

Answers

		Questions	Answers
1		Rubella is a disease, also called what?	*German measles*
2		How many cards are there in each suit of a set of playing cards?	*13*
3		In which country did the Industrial Revolution begin in the 1700s?	*Great Britain*
4		On which part of the body is the biceps?	*The upper arm (muscle)*
5		Where do lugworms live?	*In mud by the seashore*
6		Which part of a fraction is the denominator?	*The lower half*
7		True or false: engineers using high-pressure tools can turn copper into gold?	*False*
8		"Rheumatoid" is a type of which bone ailment?	*Arthritis*
9		What did Percy Shaw invent in 1934, which are seen on roads all over the world?	*Cats' eyes*
10		What is made by baking dough?	*Bread*
11		What is at the center of our Solar System?	*The Sun*
12		What sort of vessel travels on a cushion of air?	*A hovercraft*
13		What type of medical professional removes plaque?	*A dentist or dental hygienist*
14		On which continent would you find llamas?	*South America*
15		True or false: men have more wisdom teeth than women?	*False; both have four*

Quiz 66
Question 9

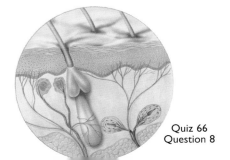

Quiz 66
Question 8

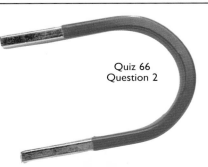

Quiz 66
Question 2

Quiz 66 Level 2

Questions

Answers

1. True or false: scientists have found written messages on the surface of the Moon? — *False*

2. What comes in varieties called bar, horseshoe, and electro? — *Magnets*

3. Which was the last planet to be discovered? — *Pluto, in 1930*

4. How many weeks are there in five years? — *260*

5. When water reaches its boiling point, what does it become? — *Steam (water vapor)*

6. Which itchy condition, caused by a fungus, usually affects the area between the toes? — *Athlete's foot*

7. What navigational device uses a magnet suspended or floated in a liquid? — *A magnetic compass*

8. What does a dermatologist study? — *The skin*

9. What name is given to the hairs on a paintbrush? — *Bristles*

10. Where is the spinal cord? — *In your backbone*

11. True or false: special underwater telescopes can provide the clearest images of the Sun? — *False*

12. What is the fastest land animal over a distance of a mile? — *A thoroughbred horse*

13. What is 20% of 20? — *4*

14. True or false: driving a car in reverse saves on gasoline? — *False*

15. In which ocean does the Gulf Stream flow? — *The Atlantic*

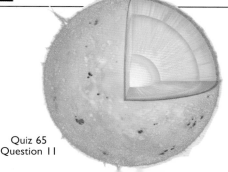

Quiz 65
Question 11

Quiz 65
Question 10

Quiz 67 Level 2

Questions

Answers

		Questions	Answers
1		What device for seeing distant objects has a name that means for both eyes?	*Binoculars*
2		What is a dingo?	*A wild dog of Australia*
3		What fruit fell on Isaac Newton's head causing him to consider gravity?	*An apple*
4		What is a stickleback?	*A type of fish*
5		What is another name for a shooting star?	*A meteor*
6		If a car is traveling at 60 mph, how far will it go in 15 minutes?	*15 miles*
7		What does a barometer measure?	*The pressure of the atmosphere*
8		True or false: biologists have developed redwood trees that can grow in the Sahara?	*False*
9		What is 25% of 16?	*4*
10		Which type of insect usually passes the disease malaria on to humans?	*Mosquito*
11		What type of animals are described as "equine"?	*Horses and their relatives*
12		What covers more than two thirds of the world's surface?	*Water*
13		What device for measuring time uses running sand?	*Hour-glass*
14		The core of the Earth is made of nickel and which other element?	*Iron*
15		Is baking powder a type of acid or alkali?	*Alkali (the opposite of acid)*

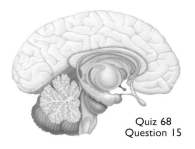

Quiz 68
Question 15

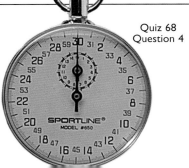

Quiz 68
Question 4

Quiz 68 Level 2

Questions

Answers

#	Question	Answer
1	True or false: the people of Iceland get most of their hot water from hot springs?	*True*
2	In a group of 100 people, how many people are likely to be left-handed?	*Ten*
3	What is 40% of 40?	*16*
4	What kind of watch is used to time a race?	*A stopwatch*
5	The gray squirrel is native to which continent?	*North America*
6	Within 2 minutes, how long does light take to reach us from the Sun?	*Eight minutes*
7	What process causes sounds to be recorded on tape such as cassettes?	*Magnetism*
8	The science which studies the history of the Earth's crust is called what?	*Geology*
9	If a wheel has a circumference of 4 feet, how many turns will it take to go 100 feet?	*25*
10	How many Great Lakes are there in North America?	*Five*
11	The initials WWF are the short name of which international organization that protects animals?	*The World Wide Fund for Nature*
12	If someone asked you to send a hard copy, what would you need to do?	*Print out a computer file on to paper*
13	What do you call a piece of land that juts out when three of its four sides border water?	*A peninsula*
14	What parts of the body does an "ENT" specialist treat?	*Ear, nose, and throat*
15	Which part of the body does Alzheimer's disease affect?	*The brain*

Quiz 67
Question 1

Quiz 67
Question 13

Quiz 69 Level 2

Questions | Answers

#	Question	Answer
1	On which continent would you find prairie dogs?	*North America*
2	What is a crevasse?	*A narrow gap in a glacier or rock face*
3	What important gas did Joseph Priestley discover in 1774?	*Oxygen*
4	What item of clothing shares its name with the process of starting up a computer?	*Boot*
5	What is the name of the "projectile" used in badminton?	*Shuttlecock*
6	What is a pothole?	*A cave that goes straight down*
7	If a person is near-sighted, do they have trouble seeing nearby objects or objects at a distance?	*Objects at a distance*
8	How many centimeters are there in an inch?	*2.54*
9	What part of a fan pushes the air?	*The blades*
10	Which three letters would a ship's radio operator send out as an emergency call?	*SOS*
11	Which bird of prey has New World and Old World varieties?	*Vultures*
12	Which is the largest continent?	*Asia*
13	What type of biologist studies the plants and animals of the seas?	*A marine biologist*
14	What is one third squared?	*One ninth*
15	What word describes the path traveled by a body in space?	*Orbit*

Quiz 70
Question 9

Quiz 70
Question 8

Quiz 70 Level 2

Questions

Answers

		Question	Answer
1		Which of the planets is nearest the sun?	*Mercury*
2		Where do musk oxen live?	*In the far north, in the Arctic region*
3		Which group of people take the Hippocratic Oath before they can begin their career?	*Doctors*
4		Which blood vessels take blood from the heart to the different parts of the body?	*Arteries*
5		What kind of reptile, famous for walking slowly, can live to be 150 years old?	*Tortoise*
6		Who invented the first battery?	*Alessandro Volta in 1800*
7		What type of thick woodland near the Equator is hot and humid all the time?	*A rain forest*
8		Which bird, native to New Zealand, shares its name with a fruit?	*Kiwi*
9		What do the British call a wrench?	*A spanner*
10	$\sqrt{x}$	A kilogram is roughly 2.2 pounds. How many pounds are there in 15 kg?	*33*
11		Taste bud cells distinguish four basic flavors, sweet, sour, bitter, and what?	*Salty*
12		What would a zoologist study?	*Animals*
13		Most cars have how many gears for going forward?	*Four or five*
14		A problem with which organ can cause people to lose their balance?	*The ear*
15		If a material is said to be ductile, what can be done to it?	*It can be drawn into thin wires*

Quiz 69
Question 5

Quiz 69
Question 4

Quiz 69
Question 9

Quiz 71 Level 2

Questions

Answers

#	Question	Answer
1	What is an elver?	*A young eel*
2	What do rivets join together?	*Pieces of metal*
3	The iris is part of which organ?	*The eye*
4	Which other Australian animal resembles a wallaby?	*Kangaroo*
5	What are the three states of matter?	*Solid, liquid, and gas*
6	Which type of climate receives more rainfall, semiarid or temperate?	*Temperate*
7	Turbot, flounder, and marlin are all examples of which type of animal?	*Fish*
8	Two knobs on a sound system adjust the pitch. One is the bass; what is the other?	*Treble*
9	What hard seed grows on a palm tree?	*Coconut*
10	What type of circles are concentric?	*Those with the same center*
11	What method of joining metals heats them until they melt and mix together?	*Welding*
12	The explorer Robert Peary became the first person to reach which place in 1909?	*The North Pole*
13	A diagonal line drawn between two corners of a square produces which two shapes?	*Two right-angled triangles*
14	Is there more land north or south of the Equator?	*North*
15	Which type of blood vessels take blood from differents part of the body back to the heart?	*Veins*

Quiz 72
Question 9

Quiz 72
Question 7

Quiz 72
Question 12

Quiz 72 Level 2

Questions

Answers

#	Question	Answer
1	Does a line of longitude run north-south or east-west across a map?	*North-south*
2	The zeppelin built in 1900 was the first successful example of what kind of craft?	*The first rigid controllable airship*
3	What does a vacuum flask do to liquids?	*Keeps them hot or cool*
4	Eating too much of a fat called cholesterol can lead to what type of disease?	*Heart disease*
5	A hexagon has how many sides?	*Six*
6	Which is the smallest continent?	*Australia*
7	The optic nerves lead to the brain from where?	*The eyes*
8	What type of scientist would provide information about an occluded front?	*A meteorologist (weather person)*
9	If you are given one playing card, what is the probability of getting an ace?	*1/13*
10	What word describes the information used by a computer?	*Data*
11	Cirrus, cumulus, and nimbus are all types of what?	*Cloud*
12	What is the probability of getting a domino with seven dots on it?	*3/28*
13	75% saltpeter, 15% charcoal, and 10% sulfur make up which substance?	*Gunpowder*
14	What type of engineer would design and build roads, bridges, and tunnels?	*A civil engineer*
15	How many grams are there in 2 kg?	*2,000*

Quiz 71
Question 9

Quiz 71
Question 7

Quiz 73 Level 3

Questions

Answers

		Questions	Answers
1		What is the capital of Ontario, Canada?	*Toronto*
2		What is a thrombosis?	*A clot in a blood vessel*
3		What is fishing with a large bag-shaped net dragged along the bottom of the sea called?	*Trawling*
4		What metal is used mainly to fuel nuclear reactors?	*Uranium*
5		Which material is used mostly for making transistors?	*Silicon*
6		What kind of stories did Jules Verne and H.G. Wells write?	*Science fiction*
7		What are the epidermis and the dermis?	*Layers of the skin*
8		What game do the British call noughts and crosses?	*Tic-tac-toe*
9		Where is your thyroid?	*In your neck*
10		What is another name for the longest day of the year?	*The summer solstice*
11		What is the name for animals that eat only plants?	*Herbivores*
12		What is Easter Island famous for?	*Its strange stone heads*
13		What is similar to a porpoise, but has a beak-like snout and swims farther from land?	*A dolphin*
14		Who commanded the victorious Union forces at the end of the U.S. Civil War?	*General Ulysses S. Grant*
15		Who was Tarzan's girlfriend?	*Jane*

Quiz 74
Question 8

Quiz 74
Question 1

Quiz 74
Question 15

Quiz 74 Level 3

Questions

Answers

#	Question	Answer
1	Which country has borders with Canada and Mexico?	*The United States*
2	Where would you find a proton?	*At the center of an atom*
3	What is the main product of Kuwait?	*Oil*
4	Which region includes parts of Norway, Sweden, Finland, and Russia?	*Lapland*
5	What is a loop of electrical conductors called?	*An electrical circuit*
6	What is the name of food prepared according to Jewish law?	*Kosher*
7	What is particularly prominent in the proboscis monkey?	*Its nose*
8	What country's national symbol is the harp?	*Ireland*
9	In which stroke do swimmers begin races in the water?	*Backstroke*
10	What is a smaller form of kangaroo usually called?	*A wallaby*
11	How many stars did the first U.S. flag have?	*13*
12	Where is the seat of government of the Netherlands?	*The Hague*
13	In which year did the Great Depression begin?	*1929*
14	In which book did Long John Silver feature?	*Treasure Island*
15	What are felines?	*Cats*

Quiz 73
Question 9

Quiz 73
Question 12

Quiz 75 Level 3

Questions

Answers

		Questions	Answers
1		Who was Plato?	*A famous Greek philosopher*
2		Which is the largest building on the Acropolis in Athens?	*The Parthenon*
3		Which sweet substance is used in the diet of diabetics and weight watchers?	*Saccharin*
4		The sap of which tree is called latex?	*The rubber tree*
5		How does sound reach our ears?	*It is carried by vibrations*
6		What is the average thickness of the Antarctic ice—60 feet, 600 feet, or 6,000 feet?	*6,000 feet*
7		Who was the first pope?	*St. Peter*
8		What is a table tennis ball made of?	*Celluloid*
9		What do we mean when we say: *Don't put all your eggs in one basket*?	*Don't rely on one thing*
10		In which state is Monument Valley?	*Utah*
11		What is the capital of Cuba?	*Havana*
12		Which U.S. state is the farthest east?	*Maine*
13		Who was Ned Kelly?	*An Australian outlaw*
14		What kind of creature is an avocet?	*A wading bird*
15		Which city is famous for its cable cars?	*San Francisco*

Quiz 76
Question 7

Quiz 76
Question 2

Quiz 76 Level 3

Questions

Answers

#	Question	Answer
1	What is 100 degrees Celsius on the Fahrenheit scale?	*212 degrees*
2	What is the architectural name for a grotesque carved head designed to catch rainwater?	*A gargoyle*
3	What was the name of the census carried out in England by William the Conqueror?	*The Domesday Book*
4	What is a digital image generated from an equation called?	*A fractal*
5	In which direction would you look for the Sun at midday in the Southern Hemisphere?	*North*
6	On what date is St. Patrick's Day?	*March 17*
7	What are these all varieties of: broccoli, brussels sprouts, and cauliflower?	*Cabbage*
8	Which poet wrote "The Wreck of the Hesperus" and "The Song of Hiawatha"?	*Longfellow*
9	What is the capital of Chile?	*Santiago*
10	Hades was the Greek god of what?	*The Underworld*
11	What is the measurement and mapping of the Earth's surface called?	*Surveying*
12	What do you use to turn sound waves into small electric currents so they can be recorded?	*A microphone*
13	What does *steal a march* on someone mean?	*Gain advantage*
14	Where are a grasshopper's ears?	*In its knees*
15	What are vertebrae?	*Bones in your backbone*

Quiz 75
Question 10

Quiz 77 Level 3

#	Question	Answer
1	Manila is the chief port and capital of which country?	*The Philippines*
2	Who discovered penicillin?	*Alexander Fleming*
3	When is a person illiterate?	*When they can't read or write*
4	Which Dutch painter produced about 60 self-portraits and painted *The Night Watch*?	*Rembrandt*
5	Which is the largest member of the cat family?	*The Siberian tiger*
6	Who wrote *Waverley*, *Rob Roy*, and *The Heart of Midlothian*?	*Walter Scott*
7	What is the capital of Finland?	*Helsinki*
8	Which Russian czar was called "the Terrible"?	*Ivan IV*
9	What kind of boat skims across the surface of the water on underwater wings?	*A hydrofoil*
10	The trunk of which tree swells in wet weather and shrinks in dry weather?	*The baobab tree*
11	What is two-thirds written as a decimal?	*0.666 repeating (0.67)*
12	What do doctors use to inject drugs into the body?	*A hypodermic needle*
13	What kind of stone did early people use to make tools and weapons?	*Flint*
14	What are the largest pieces of land on Earth called?	*Continents*
15	Which metal makes the strongest magnets?	*Iron*

Quiz 78
Question 15

Quiz 78 Level 3

1	How do pythons and anacondas kill their prey?	*By squeezing and suffocating it*
2	What part of the body does a podiatrist treat?	*The feet*
3	In which city is the Kremlin?	*Moscow*
4	Did dinosaurs lay eggs?	*Yes, like all reptiles*
5	Who was the first European to explore the coasts of Australia and New Zealand?	*Captain James Cook*
6	What type of tennis courts is Wimbledon famous for?	*Grass courts*
7	What is the name for all the bodies that orbit the Sun and the Sun itself?	*The Solar System*
8	What is the name of a word made by rearranging the letters of another word?	*Anagram*
9	What is the name for the stone at the top of an arch which locks the whole arch together?	*The keystone*
10	Who wrote *The Ugly Duckling*?	*Hans Christian Andersen*
11	In which country is the huge rock known as Uluru?	*Australia*
12	Which is the smallest prime number?	*1*
13	Which U.S. President had talks with the Soviet Union which led to the end of the Cold War?	*Ronald Reagan*
14	Why does the Sun look the same size as the Moon although many millions of times bigger?	*Because it is much farther away*
15	Where are the Northwest Territories?	*Canada*

Quiz 77
Question 9

Quiz 77
Question 5

Quiz 79 Level 3

1		Which kind of heavenly body is made of very hot gas and gives out heat and light?	*A star*
2		Who is head of the Church of England?	*The king or queen of Great Britain*
3		What is the name for a creature that eats all kinds of food, both plants and animals?	*An omnivore*
4		What does humidity measure?	*The amount of water in the air*
5		In which state is Harvard University?	*Massachusetts*
6		How many pairs of wings does a fly have?	*2*
7		What is another name for a capsicum?	*A pepper*
8		How did *Stegosaurus* defend itself?	*It had thick, bony plates, like armor*
9		Which Indian city produces more films than Hollywood?	*Bombay*
10		Which country has the second-largest population in the world?	*India*
11		Where does the jaguar live?	*In the forests of South America*
12		What is a kibbutz?	*A collective farm in Israel*
13		Which country is Beirut the capital of?	*Lebanon*
14		The people of which ancient civilization spilled a drop of blood every morning to please their gods?	*The Aztecs*
15		What is the square of 11?	*121*

Quiz 80
Question 14

Quiz 80
Question 8

Quiz 80 Level 3

1	Does Mars have any moons?	*Yes (2—Deimos and Phobos)*
2	What lies under the ice at the North Pole?	*Sea*
3	What is a *stage whisper*?	*One that everyone can hear*
4	Which grassland animal digs interlinking underground burrows?	*The prairie dog*
5	Where is the Cape of Good Hope?	*At the southern tip of Africa*
6	Who wrote *The Pilgrim's Progress*?	*John Bunyan*
7	How did Marie Antoinette die during the French Revolution?	*She was guillotined*
8	Who was Norma Jean Baker?	*Marilyn Monroe*
9	Which country was ruled by czars?	*Russia*
10	What do whales feed their young on?	*Milk (they are mammals)*
11	Which king signed the Magna Carta?	*King John*
12	Of which religion is the Torah the holy book?	*Judaism*
13	Which is the only metal that is liquid at room temperature?	*Mercury*
14	Doric, Ionic, and Corinthian are all what?	*Orders of architecture*
15	What is the capital of Iraq?	*Baghdad*

Quiz 79
Question 6

Quiz 79
Question 7

Quiz 81 Level 3

1	Which sea creatures swim by squirting out water through a tube?	*Squids and octopuses*
2	Which famous baseball field is known as "the house that Ruth built"?	*Yankee Stadium*
3	Which river runs alongside Washington, D.C.?	*The Potomac*
4	Who landed in Britain in 55BC?	*Julius Caesar*
5	How many wings does a dragonfly have?	*4*
6	Which sea is really the world's largest lake?	*The Caspian Sea*
7	Who is the American state of Virginia named after?	*Queen Elizabeth I, the Virgin Queen*
8	How many square meters are there in a hectare?	*10,000*
9	What was the name of the fairy in *Peter Pan*?	*Tinker Bell*
10	What is the only food of vampire bats?	*Blood*
11	Which is the largest island in the Caribbean Sea?	*Cuba*
12	Athletes sometimes damage their Achilles tendon. Where is it?	*At the back of the heel*
13	What is the Roman name for Poseidon, the Greek god of the sea?	*Neptune*
14	What is the name for an area in space that sucks everything into itself, even light?	*A black hole*
15	Who was known as the "father of the U.S. Navy"?	*John Paul Jones*

Quiz 82
Question 8

Quiz 82 Level 3

#	Question	Answer
1	What force holds the Earth in its path around the Sun?	*Gravity*
2	Were there any people around when the dinosaurs lived?	*No*
3	What sort of person is called *a tower of strength*?	*A reliable, comforting person*
4	What is bauxite used for?	*Making aluminum*
5	How do camels avoid sinking into the sand?	*They have large feet*
6	What is the name of the headquarters of the US armed forces?	*The Pentagon*
7	Where did a great fire take place in 1666?	*In London*
8	Which ocean liner was said to be unsinkable but sank on its first voyage?	*The* Titanic
9	Which city is said to be built on seven hills?	*Rome*
10	What is the name for the process that turns animal skins into leather?	*Tanning*
12	What type of trees make up the largest forest in the world?	*Conifers*
11	What is a female fox called?	*Vixen*
13	What is the female of hero?	*Heroine*
14	Of which country is Kampala the capital?	*Uganda*
15	Name a disease spread by some kinds of mosquito.	*Malaria and yellow fever*

Quiz 81
Question 1

Quiz 81
Question 13

Quiz 83 Level 3

#		Question	Answer
1		Which city is called "The Big Apple"?	*New York*
2		Where are the bones the tibia, the fibula, and the femur?	*In your leg*
3		How can you tell the age of a felled tree?	*By counting the rings on its stump*
4		Which black powder is made from saltpeter, sulfur, and carbon?	*Gunpowder*
5		When do married people celebrate their golden wedding anniversary?	*After 50 years*
6		What is a macaw?	*A brightly colored parrot*
7		What word describes creatures that come out at night?	*Nocturnal*
8		Where is the earthquake danger zone known as the San Andreas Fault?	*California*
9		In which country is the Black Forest?	*Germany*
10		In which religion do boys have a bar mitzvah?	*Judaism*
11		What powered Stephenson's locomotive *Rocket*?	*Steam*
12		Which American flew a kite in a thunderstorm to prove that lightning was electricity?	*Benjamin Franklin*
13		Cereals, such as wheat, oats, and rice, are cultivated what?	*Grasses*
14		Who was Cicero?	*A famous Roman orator*
15		Which river is St. Louis built on?	*The Mississippi*

Quiz 84
Question 9

Quiz 84
Question 1

Quiz 84 Level 3

#	Question	Answer
1	Which Australian bird is also called the laughing jackass?	*The kookaburra*
2	Which sport uses the smaller ball, tennis or squash?	*Squash*
3	What is the name of the famous statue of the goddess Venus in the Louvre Museum in Paris?	*Venus de Milo*
4	Gandhi was given the name Mahatma. What does *Mahatma* mean?	*Great soul*
5	What is an ampersand?	*The character &*
6	What is ebony?	*A hard jet-black wood*
7	Which method of healing involves inserting needles into the body at certain points?	*Acupuncture*
8	*They jumped through the hoop.* Which is the verb in that sentence?	*Jumped*
9	Which planet is called the Ringed Planet?	*Saturn*
10	What did William Wallace and Robert the Bruce fight for about 700 years ago?	*Scotland's independence*
11	Which is the only creature that can turn its head in an almost complete circle?	*The owl*
12	For which service did press gangs recruit men in the early 19th century?	*The navy*
13	What is the name of the disorder caused by pollen from plants floating in the air?	*Hay fever*
14	What does NASA do?	*Launches spacecraft and satellites*
15	What won't a rolling stone gather?	*Moss*

Quiz 83
Question 11

Quiz 83
Question 6

Quiz 85 Level 3

Answers

1		Which is the highest mountain in Africa?	*Mount Kilimanjaro*
2		Where does the oxygen in the air come from?	*Plants*
3		Which country did Burke and Wills explore?	*Australia*
4		What are the wild reindeer of North America called?	*Caribou*
5		What do you get if you mix zinc and copper?	*Brass*
6		What is the capital of Argentina?	*Buenos Aires*
7		What do Frederick Ashton, Marie Rambert, and Margot Fonteyn have in common?	*Ballet*
8		Who wrote *The Canterbury Tales*?	*Geoffrey Chaucer*
9		What kind of creature is a Gila monster?	*A lizard*
10		What type of cheese is used as a pizza topping?	*Mozzarella*
11		What is 10% of 65?	*6.5*
12		What is the silent letter in rhubarb?	*H*
13		Where is the Rift Valley?	*In eastern Africa*
14		What code uses short and long signals?	*Morse code*
15		Which sport has birdies, eagles, and chips?	*Golf*

Quiz 86
Question 12

Quiz 86 Level 3

Questions

Answers

#	Question	Answer
1	How many players are there in a baseball team?	*Nine*
2	Bermuda is a colony of which country?	*Britain*
3	What is an anesthetic used for?	*To deaden pain*
4	What is the capital of New York State?	*Albany*
5	Which army destroyed the Inca empire in 1532?	*The Spanish conquistadors*
6	What are ceramics?	*Porcelain and pottery*
7	What is the name for the wearing away of the land by running water, weather, ice, and wind?	*Erosion*
8	Which animal lives on the leaves of the eucalyptus tree?	*The koala*
9	Where would you see cirrocumulus?	*In the sky; it is a type of cloud*
10	With which sport was Abner Doubleday associated?	*Baseball*
11	What does a starfish do if it loses an arm?	*It grows another one*
12	Name a prehistoric flying reptile?	*Pterodactyl*
13	"Patience" is a British name for which card game?	*Solitaire*
14	What does *play your cards close to your chest* mean?	*Not give any information away*
15	Where is Namibia?	*In southwest Africa*

Quiz 85
Question 4

Quiz 85
Question 3

Quiz 87 Level 3

Questions

Answers

#	Question	Answer
1	What nationality was the painter John Constable?	*English*
2	Who drew up the first periodic table of the chemical elements in the 1860s?	*Dmitri Mendeleyev*
3	Which artist/writer created the Cat in the Hat?	*Dr. Seuss*
4	In which year did Captain Cook begin the first of his round the world voyages: 1668, 1768, or 1868?	*1768*
5	In which country are there teachers of flower arranging called Flower Masters?	*Japan*
6	Whom did the USA fight in the war of 1812?	*Britain*
7	What musical instrument was Chopin famous for playing?	*Piano*
8	What was *Skylab*?	*The first U.S. manned space station (1973-9)*
9	Which president promised to land a "man on the Moon" by 1970?	*John F. Kennedy*
10	Where did Roald Amundsen, who beat Captain Scott to the South Pole, come from?	*Norway*
11	Which country's army won the battle of Sedan in 1870?	*Germany (defeating France)*
12	From which ancient language do we get the word "politics"?	*Greek*
13	Which nation did the Greeks defeat after a long war in 479BC?	*The Persians*
14	What is a dagger with a very fine, slender blade called?	*A stiletto*
15	In 1897 it was discovered that which insect causes malaria?	*Mosquito*

Quiz 88
Question 6

Quiz 88
Question 5

Quiz 88
Question 2

Quiz 88 Level 3

Questions   Answers

#	Question	Answer
1	In which sport was Knut Rockne a famous coach: football, boxing, or cricket?	*Football*
2	What was a V-2?	*A German rocket of World War II*
3	What was the world land speed record in 1906: 78 mph, 98 mph, or 128 mph?	*128 mph*
4	Old maps show *Terra Australis Incognita*—what did this mean?	*Unknown Southern Continent, in Latin*
5	Who was made Lord Protector, and ruled England after the Civil War?	*Oliver Cromwell*
6	In which film series, started in 1977, do C-3PO and R2-D2 appear?	**Star Wars**
7	Which war was called "the war to end all wars"?	*World War I (1914-1918)*
8	When did Russians begin exploring Siberia: 1500s, 1800s, or 1900s?	*1500s*
9	Soldiers from which army were able to form a defensive "tortoise" with their shields?	*Roman*
10	In 1710 the first model was built that showed how the planets moved. What was it called?	*An orrery*
11	In which country is the Muslim holy city of Mecca?	**Saudi Arabia**
12	The Library of Congress was founded in 1800 in which country?	*The USA*
13	Where did Robert Clive find fame and fortune in the 1700s?	*India*
14	What kind of races took place in the Circus Maximus in Rome?	*Chariot races*
15	Which planet was visited by the *Galileo* probe in 1995?	*Jupiter*

Quiz 87
Question 7

Quiz 87
Question 15

Quiz 89 Level 3

Questions

Answers

#	Question	Answer
1	In which war did British troops recapture Port Stanley?	*Falklands War (1982)*
2	Who served as U.S. president before George Bush Sr.?	*Ronald Reagan*
3	Which organization, that uses the initials RNLI, was founded in 1824?	*Royal National Lifeboat Institution*
4	Which war was fought in Asia from 1950 to 1953?	*Korean War*
5	Who discovered that blood circulates around the body?	*William Harvey*
6	Was the Battle of Midway (1942) fought at sea or on land?	*At sea*
7	What is Louis-Antoine de Bougainville's claim to fame?	*He led the first French voyage around the world*
8	Which writer created both Mr. Pickwick and Ebenezer Scrooge?	*Charles Dickens*
9	What instrument did Benny Goodman play?	*Clarinet*
10	By what name was T.E. Lawrence also known?	*Lawrence of Arabia*
11	What was Betsy Ross famous for?	*Making the first U.S. flag in 1776*
12	Which continent did Edward Bransfield and Nathaniel Palmer sight in 1820?	*Antarctica*
13	What was the operation called that forced Saddam Hussein out of Kuwait?	*Operation Desert Storm*
14	Who led the Third Crusade in 1189?	*Richard I*
15	What was a Patriot missile designed to shoot down?	*Other missiles*

Quiz 90
Question 11

Quiz 90
Question 14

Quiz 90 Level 3

Questions	Answers

1 What is the first letter in the Greek alphabet? — *Alpha*

2 Who was the Roman god of war? — *Mars*

3 Who was the youngest person ever to be elected U.S. president at the age of 43? — *John F. Kennedy*

4 What region of the world did Hernando de Soto explore in the 1500s? — *The American Southwest*

5 Joseph Lister first used carbolic acid to kill germs during surgery in which year: 1805, 1865, or 1895? — *1865*

6 In which country were soccer's 1998 World Cup finals held? — *France*

7 In which sport were Ayrton Senna and Jackie Stewart world champions? — *Motor racing (Grand Prix)*

8 Which people fought in regiments called impis? — *The Zulus*

9 How did sugar cane and wheat reach America in the 1500s? — *The Spanish brought them*

10 Where is the Khyber Pass, scene of a famous 19th-century massacre? — *Afghanistan-Pakistan border*

11 What form of transportation, invented by the Chinese, was a junk? — *A sailing ship*

12 Which actress married Prince Rainier of Monaco before being killed in a car accident in 1982? — *Grace Kelly*

13 In which century did the Russian composer Piotr Tchaikovsky live? — *19th century (1840–1893)*

14 Which type of planes competed for the Schneider Trophy? — *Sea planes*

15 The Romans believed they had to travel across a river to the afterlife. What was the river called? — *River Styx*

Quiz 89
Question 3

Quiz 89
Question 14

Quiz 91 Level 3

Questions

Answers

		Questions	Answers
1		What city was split between the Allies after World War II?	*Berlin*
2	?	Which country is also known as Hellas?	*Greece*
3		Which two countries fought the Opium War of 1839?	*Britain and China*
4		What was El Dorado?	*A mythical city of gold in South America*
5	?	Where was the ancient city of Carthage?	*Near modern Tunis, in north Africa*
6		Which king gave up the British throne in 1936?	*Edward VIII (later Duke of Windsor)*
7		Who won the battle of New Orleans in 1815?	*The Americans (beating the British)*
8		After whom is Frobisher Bay in Canada named?	*The English explorer Martin Frobisher*
9		Which two Middle Eastern countries were at war from 1980 to 1988?	*Iran and Iraq*
10		In which Irish city was James Joyce's novel, *Ulysses*, set?	*Dublin*
11	?	The sedan chair originated in Italy and arrived in England in 1634. What is it?	*A single enclosed seat carried on poles*
12	?	On which continent did people look for King Solomon's Mines?	*Africa*
13		What "first ever" did Matthew Webb achieve in 1875?	*He swam the English Channel*
14		The Black Death reached England in 1348. What was the Black Death?	*An epidemic of bubonic plague*
15	?	Which festive bird came to European tables from America in the 1500s?	*The turkey*

Quiz 92
Question 6

Quiz 92 Level 3

Questions

Answers

#	Question	Answer
1	What kind of aircraft, first built in 1939 by Igor Sikorsky, has rotor blades?	*A helicopter*
2	In 1610 Henry Hudson sailed into Hudson Bay: but where did he think he was?	*The Pacific Ocean*
3	Which sport uses racquets and was invented in England in the 1800s?	*Tennis*
4	Which king built a huge palace and church called the Escorial?	*Philip II of Spain*
5	Which continent did Mungo Park explore in the early 1800s?	*Africa*
6	About which French invasion of Russia did Tchaikovsky compose a piece of music?	*Napoleon's invasion in 1812*
7	Where did the U.S. *Pathfinder* spacecraft land in July 1997?	*Mars*
8	Which is the world's biggest glider, first used in 1982?	*The U.S. space shuttle*
9	Which 17th-century English poet continued writing after he became blind?	*John Milton*
10	Which North African city was first visited by Europeans in the 1820s?	*Timbuktu*
11	In which country did the Satsuma Rebellion occur?	*Japan (1877)*
12	Who was known as "the Iron Chancellor"?	*Otto von Bismarck*
13	Who wrote *Uncle Tom's Cabin*?	*Harriet Beecher Stowe*
14	Who made the first solo round-the-world-flight?	*Wiley Post (1933)*
15	When did the U.S. adopt the "Star Spangled Banner" as the national anthem?	*March 3, 1931*

Quiz 91
Question 11

Quiz 93 Level 3

Questions

Answers

		Question	Answer
1		When did the last Ice Age end: 1 million, 10,000, or 1,000 years ago?	*10,000 years ago*
2		Who fought against Rome in the Punic wars?	*Carthage*
3		What were aqueducts used for in ancient Rome?	*Bringing water*
4		What kind of gun was the Colt 45?	*A revolver*
5		Who is the father of Britain's princes William and Harry?	*Charles, Prince of Wales*
6		Which plane first flew in July 1989?	*B-2 Spirit stealth bomber*
7		In which country does the story of the opera *Madam Butterfly* take place?	*Japan*
8		Who was the most famous European explorer in Africa?	*David Livingstone*
9		In which war did Montgomery and Patton become famous generals?	*World War II (1939-1945)*
10		Who wrote the music for the opera *Porgy and Bess* in 1935?	*George Gershwin*
11		Of which international organization did Kofi Annan become Secretary General in 1997?	*United Nations*
12		Who commanded the army that beat the French at Waterloo in 1815?	*The Duke of Wellington*
13		How old was Alexander the Great when he died: 33, 53, or 63?	*33*
14		In 1863 James Speke discovered the source of the world's longest river; which river?	*The Nile*
15		Which sort of scanning did Ian Donal develop in the 1950s?	*Ultrasound*

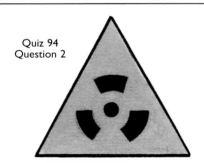

Quiz 94
Question 2

Quiz 94
Question 12

Quiz 94 Level 3

Questions

Answers

		Question	Answer
1		Which great Italian city was sacked by the Goths in AD410?	*Rome*
2		The Geiger counter was invented in 1913 to measure what?	*Radioactivity*
3		Which African river did Henry Morton Stanley explore in the 1870s?	*The Congo*
4		Which Australian tennis star was nicknamed "The Rockhampton Rocket"?	*Rod Laver*
5		Are reptiles' eggs hard-shelled, or leathery?	*Leathery*
6		Were helicopters used in World War I?	*No: they were not used in war until the 1940s*
7		Which arabic sailor featured in *The Arabian Nights*?	*Sinbad*
8		Who was called the father of psychoanalysis?	*Sigmund Freud*
9		How did the explorers Burke and Wills meet their deaths?	*They starved to death in Australia*
10		Was Calamity Jane a real person?	*Yes: her real name was Martha Jane Canary*
11		Which type of sport is Wimbledon famous for?	*Tennis*
12		In 1090, the Chinese built the Cosmic Engine. Did it measure time, rainfall, or plant growth?	*Time; it was an early mechanical clock*
13		What nationality was World War I's General Haig?	*British*
14		Which is the biggest selling car of all time?	*The Volkswagen Beetle*
15		Which Norwegian artist painted *The Scream*?	*Edvard Munch*

Quiz 93
Question 8

Quiz 93
Question 6

Quiz 95 Level 3

Questions

Answers

		Questions		Answers
1		What was the main Viking weapon, apart from the sword and spear?	Quiz 96 Question 7	The battleax
2		Of which country was François Mitterand leader?		France
3		Which inventor was called "The Wizard of Menlo Park"?		Edison (Menlo Park was the site of his laboratory)
4		Where did soldiers wear armor called greaves?		On their shins
5		The sinking of the USS *Maine* in 1898 triggered which war?		The Spanish-American War
6		The world's first civilization was "the land between two rivers." What do we call it?		Mesopotamia
7		Avicenna was a famous Persian doctor, writer, or soldier?		Doctor
8		What name was given to a Norse warrior wearing bearskins who went crazy in battle?		A berserker
9		The first Chinese emperor was buried with an army of life-size soldiers. What were they made of?		Terracotta
10		What kind of aircraft was the World War II Catalina?		A flying boat
11		What was Edison's kinetoscope?		A peephole machine, for watching short films
12		When was the first armored car built?		1904
13		In which sport did Carl Lewis become a star?		Track and field
14		On which planet did the *Venera 7* space probe land in 1970?		Venus
15		Which Welsh poet wrote *Under Milk Wood*?		Dylan Thomas

Quiz 96
Question 2

Quiz 96 Level 3

Questions | Answers

#	Question	Answer
1	What kind of lamp did Joseph Swan invent?	*The electric lamp*
2	Which great London cathedral was completed in 1717?	*St. Paul's Cathedral*
3	Who was U.S. president for most of World War II?	*Franklin D. Roosevelt*
4	What kind of fish was the star of the *Jaws* films?	*A great white shark*
5	What weapon was fixed to the bow of an ancient Egyptian warship?	*A ram for sinking enemy ships*
6	What were the main divisions of the Roman army called?	*Legions*
7	Which people were probably the first Europeans to "discover" America?	*The Vikings*
8	The powerful ancient "composite" bow was made of wood, animal sinew, and what?	*Horn*
9	What garment did a Roman man drape over his tunic?	*A toga*
10	Could Abraham Lincoln have met George Washington?	*No: Washington died before Lincoln was born*
11	Who wrote horror tales such as *The Fall of the House of Usher*?	*Edgar Allan Poe*
12	Which modern country made up most of Gaul in Roman times?	*France*
13	What nationality was the physicist Hans Christian Oersted (1777-1851)?	*Danish*
14	Which hunting weapon used by Australian aboriginals was also used by ancient Egyptians?	*The boomerang*
15	Did the coffee plant originally grow wild in Africa or South America?	*Africa*

Quiz 95
Question 10

Quiz 95
Question 14

Quiz 97 Level 3

Questions

Answers

#	Question	Answer
1	In which war did the city of Saigon fall?	The Vietnam War
2	Of which country was Golda Meir a famous leader?	Israel
3	Of what was Sir George Cayley (1753-1857) a pioneer?	Flight (he built experimental gliders)
4	Who or what were fighter aces?	Pilots who shot down many enemy planes
5	Was the jitterbug a dance or a disease?	A dance popular in the 1940s
6	Who built an early steamship called the *Clermont*?	Robert Fulton
7	What did Dick Rutan and Jeanna Yeager do in nine days in 1986?	Flew round the world without refueling
8	"Once more into the breach dear friends" were words attributed to King Henry V by whom?	William Shakespeare
9	Who wrote *Robinson Crusoe*?	Daniel Defoe
10	The Roman gladiator called a *retiarius* fought with a net and which other weapon?	A trident
11	When did people first wear nylon clothing: 1930s, 1950s, or 1970s?	1930s
12	Who wiped out three Roman legions in the Teutoburger forest in AD9?	German tribes
13	Who was married to the Empress Josephine?	Napoleon Bonaparte
14	In which books does a wizard called Gandalf appear?	The Hobbit *and* The Lord of the Rings
15	Which Queen Mary was executed in 1587?	Mary Queen of Scots

Quiz 98
Question 2

Quiz 98
Question 10

Quiz 98 Level 3

Questions

Answers

		Question	Answer
1		Where does the curious crawling parrot called the kakapo live?	*New Zealand*
2		Who was the 19th-century founder of Communism?	*Karl Marx*
3		Which of Shakespeare's plays is about a noble Moor?	Othello
4		Which are the biggest and most powerful warships today?	*Aircraft carriers*
5		Captain Cook fed his crew on "sour krout": what was it? *Quiz 97 Question 8*	*Cabbage pickled in vinegar*
6		Did eating too many potatoes make King Henry VIII so fat?	*No. He died before they reached England*
7		Which medical instrument for listening to the sounds of the chest was invented in 1819?	*The stethoscope*
8		Against whom was Robert the Bruce fighting when he was inspired to try again by a spider?	*King Edward II of England*
9		What was the name of the short, stabbing sword used by the Roman soldiers?	*Gladius*
10		What was special about the dinosaur called *stegosaurus*?	*It had jagged plates on its back*
11		Renoir, Rembrandt, and Reynolds were all . . . what?	*Painters*
12		Why did sailing warships have copper bottoms?	*To stop seaworms boring holes in the wood*
13		John Hunter was an important figure in which field of medicine?	*Surgery*
14		What was the Crystal Palace?	*A huge glass and steel building (London 1851)*
15		Which country developed the first atomic bomb?	*The United States*

Quiz 97
Question 15

Quiz 97
Question 13

Quiz 99 Level 3

Questions

Answers

		Questions	Answers
1		What did Native Americans do with pemmican?	*They ate it (it was dried meat)*
2		Of which country were Brian Mulroney and Pierre Trudeau prime ministers?	*Canada*
3		Why did Joseph Lister use carbolic acid in operating rooms?	*To kill germs and prevent infection*
4		Stephen Crane wrote *The Red Badge of Courage:* about which war?	*The American Civil War*
5		Which baseball stadium, built in 1912, has the "Green Monster"?	*Fenway Park (Red Sox)*
6		Which one of these was invented in the 18th century: steam vehicle, radio, microscope?	*Steam vehicle*
7		Who was it that was restored in the "Restoration" in England in 1660?	*Charles II (to the throne of England)*
8		What did sailors use hammocks for?	*They slept in them*
9		A tower in Paris is named after him; he also designed the skeleton for the Statue of Liberty. What was his name?	*Alexandre Eiffel*
10		Which unit of power, invented by James Watt, measures the output of an engine?	*Horsepower*
11		Who led a peasants' rebellion in England in 1381?	*Wat Tyler*
12		In what year was the first "test-tube" baby born?	*1978*
13		Why was there fighting in India in 1857?	*It was the year of the Indian Mutiny*
14		Which was the only dinosaur to have three horns?	Triceratops
15		Which composer wrote the *Young Person's Guide to the Orchestra*?	*Benjamin Britten*

Quiz 100
Question 6

Quiz 100
Question 15

Quiz 100 Level 3

Questions

Answers

#	Question	Answer
1	Which pop stars made a film called *A Hard Day's Night*?	The Beatles
2	Where did Peary and Henson go in 1909?	Portugal
3	Who was Geronimo?	An Apache Indian Chief
4	With what invention is Robert Oppenheimer (1904-1967) associated?	The atomic bomb
5	Which Christian saint was sent by the Pope to convert the English in AD597?	Augustine
6	Which was the most important British fighter plane to be used in the Battle of Britain?	The Hurricane
7	Of which country is David the patron saint?	Wales
8	How many labors did Hercules have to perform?	Twelve
9	How many shots could a musket fire before being reloaded?	One
10	In the Bible, who was thrown into a lion's den for defying King Nebuchadnezzar?	Daniel
11	Of what country was Henry the Navigator a prince (in the 1400s)?	Portugal
12	With which rock group did Mick Jagger find fame?	The Rolling Stones
13	Who composed the *William Tell Overture*?	Rossini
14	What is the ancient Japanese art of bonsai?	Growing miniature trees
15	Of which country was Mussolini leader from 1922 to 1943?	Italy

Quiz 99
Question 7

Quiz 99
Question 14

Quiz 101 Level 3

Questions

Answers

		Question	Answer
1		What do you call four children born to the same mother at the same time?	*Quadruplets*
2		Which sense do hedgehogs rely on to find their food?	*Smell*
3		Which is the smallest planet?	*Pluto*
4		What is a skink?	*A type of lizard*
5		Which of the following is a prime number? 12, 21, 31, 39, 49?	*31*
6		What has happened to a bone that is fractured?	*It has broken*
7		What occurs when the moon lies in front of the Sun?	*A solar eclipse*
8		What type of doctor would operate on the cerebellum?	*A brain surgeon*
9		The piano is a percussion instrument: true or false?	*True*
10		On which planet did the Pathfinder mission land in 1966?	*Mars*
11		Bread mold is closely related to which important medicine?	*Penicillin*
12		What type of angle is described as being acute?	*One that is smaller than a right angle*
13		On a ship, what is the screw?	*The propeller*
14		The epidermis is the outer layer of what?	*The skin*
15		What kind of pink bird can grow up to 5 feet?	*Flamingo*

Quiz 102
Question 3

Quiz 102
Question 14

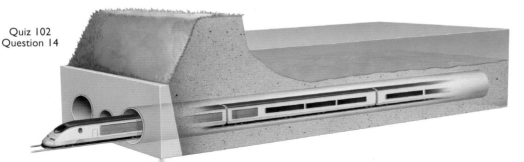

Quiz 102 Level 3

Questions

Answers

1		What is the fruit of an oak tree called?	*An acorn*
2		What type of body tissue expands and relaxes in order to let people move?	*Muscle*
3		If a mathematician is using a protractor, what is she or he measuring?	*Angles*
4		What type of device throws the image of a film onto a screen?	*A projector*
5		What is the name of the large island that lies off the southeast coast of Africa?	*Madagascar*
6		Which grow to be longer, crocodiles or alligators?	*Crocodiles (the Asian and Australian type)*
7		What is produced by a solar cell?	*Electricity*
8		What metal is used to galvanize steel or iron?	*Zinc*
9		Complete the following: 4:12 as 6:?	*18*
10		What are the three primary colors of light?	*Red, blue, and green*
11		Which river has two branches known as the White and the Blue?	*The Nile*
12		If a wheel turns two times, how many degrees has it traveled?	*720*
13		If a disease is hereditary, how does someone catch it?	*It is inherited from one or both parents*
14		Which famous length of railroad passes between Folkestone, England and Calais, France?	*The Channel Tunnel*
15		Centigrade is another name for which measurement?	*Celsius (temperature)*

Quiz 103 Level 3

Questions | ## Answers

#		Question	Answer
1		What do you call a small piece of wood, glass, or metal that gets stuck in the skin?	*A splinter*
2		How many inches are there in 15 feet?	*180*
3		Into which body of water does the Danube River empty?	*The Black Sea*
4		The average roomful of air weighs 33, 55, 77, or 100 pounds?	*100 pounds*
5		What small computer storage device was introduced in 1970?	*The floppy disk*
6		What do the letters DC stand for in electricity?	*Direct current*
7		Which group of mammals share their name with a kind of tooth?	*Canines*
8		What lens touches the cornea when worn?	*Contact lens*
9		Which word describes an inward-curving surface, like the inside of a bowl?	*Concave*
10		What do you call a constantly rolling staircase?	*An escalator*
11		Who are more likely to suffer from color blindness, men or women?	*Men*
12		How many hours have you slept if you fell asleep at 2015 and woke at 0745?	*Eleven and a half*
13		What radioactive element was discovered by the German Martin Klaproth in 1841?	*Uranium*
14		What do you call the spiral lines running down a screw?	*The thread*
15		Which fruit was once known as the Chinese gooseberry?	*The kiwi fruit*

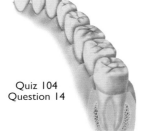

Quiz 104
Question 14

Quiz 104
Question 1

Quiz 104 Level 3

Questions

Answers

1	Which is the odd one out: snail, beetle, turtle, crab?	*Turtle; it is the only one with a backbone*
2	What type of injury can be either first degree, second degree, or third degree?	*Burn*
3	What is a monorail?	*A railway using one rail rather than two*
4	What do you call the longest side of a right-angled triangle?	*The hypotenuse*
5	Which river combines with the Mississippi to form one of the world's longest river systems?	*The Missouri*
6	What does a Geiger counter measure?	*Radiation (radioactivity)*
7	Where do aquatic plants live?	*In the water*
8	How many sides has a pentagon?	*Five*
9	What ape is most closely related to humans?	*Chimpanzee*
10	Galileo dropped objects from which famous building to learn about how fast things fall?	*The Leaning Tower of Pisa*
11	The Ural Mountains form part of the border between which two continents?	*Europe and Asia*
12	The word algebra comes from which language?	*Arabic*
13	Which substance makes fireworks explode?	*Gunpowder*
14	Enamel, the hardest substance in the body, is the outside covering of what?	*The teeth*
15	What is the nearest planet to the Sun?	*Mercury*

Quiz 103
Question 5

Quiz 103
Question 7

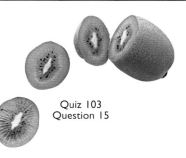

Quiz 103
Question 15

Quiz 105 Level 3

Questions

Answers

		Questions	Answers
1		What do you call an open sore on the lining of the intestine?	*An ulcer*
2		How many degrees has a quadrant?	*90 (it is one-quarter of a circle)*
3		What is sorghum?	*A grain grown in warm climates*
4		What is our galaxy called?	*The Milky Way*
5		British scientist William Fox Talbot was a pioneer in which field?	*Photography*
6		What do you call a big ship or truck that carries large amounts of liquid?	*A tanker*
7		What fruit grows in groups called "hands"?	*Bananas*
8		In which European country would you find fjords?	*Norway*
9		What cords vibrate when we talk?	*Vocal cords*
10		What is a samoyed?	*A breed of dog*
11		Which word can be added to the following to make three tools: hack, band, jig?	*Saw*
12		What man-made objects orbit the Earth and help with communication?	*Satellites*
13		What is 90% of 90?	*81*
14		What color flame is produced when a substance containing copper is burned?	*Bluish green*
15		Which uses more of the body's energy, swimming or tennis?	*Swimming*

Quiz 106
Question 6

Quiz 106
Question 15

Quiz 106 Level 3

Questions   ## Answers

#	Question	Answer
1	What is amnesia?	Loss of memory
2	What is an extinct volcano?	A volcano that no longer erupts
3	What proportion of the air is oxygen: one fifth, one eighth, or one tenth?	One fifth
4	What is 30% of 30?	9
5	What tool uses air and water to determine if something lies flat?	A spirit level
6	What kind of amphibian shares its name with a part of a horse's hoof?	A frog
7	What kind of test would an audiologist give?	A hearing test
8	Which British engineer is associated with the invention of the jet engine?	Sir Frank Whittle
9	A "supernova" is the birth of a star. True or false?	False—it is the death of a star
10	Who invented the first carpet sweeper?	Thomas Ewbank in 1889
11	How many grams are there in a ton?	One million
12	What connects the following names: Heathrow, Charles de Gaulle, Gatwick?	They are names of major airports
13	What type of animal lives in a sett?	Badger
14	Which two oceans meet at the Cape of Good Hope?	Atlantic and Indian
15	What organ in the body does a dialysis machine replace?	Kidney

Quiz 105
Question 7

Quiz 105
Question 10

Quiz 105
Question 9

Quiz 107 Level 3

Questions

Answers

#		Question	Answer
1		Which is larger, Mars or Saturn?	*Saturn*
2		In 1782 which French brothers made a flight in a hot-air balloon?	*The Montgolfier brothers*
3		The 37 species of toucan all live in which continent?	*South America*
4		In which disease do some of the body's cells go out of control and multiply?	*Cancer*
5		Which type of metal is usually measured in karats?	*Gold*
6		What aid for sailors was built at Alexandria, Egypt?	*A lighthouse*
7		Which sleek sea animal has breeding grounds called rookeries?	*Seals*
8		Which line of tropic runs through South America, Africa, and Australia?	*The Tropic of Capricorn*
9		If an engineer is measuring a moving object's RPMs, what is he or she checking?	*Revolutions per Minute*
10		What two muscles are used to lift the forearm?	*Bicep and tricep*
11		Which small weapon did Samuel Colt invent in 1835?	*The revolver*
12		A block and tackle is a group of what?	*Pulleys*
13		Which is larger, 0/4 or 0/16?	*Neither; they are both zero*
14		In which country is the famous volcano Mt. Fuji?	*Japan*
15		Which shellfish produces pearls?	*Oyster*

Quiz 108
Question 9

Quiz 108 Level 3

Questions

Answers

#	Question	Answer
1	What means of communication uses a series of dots and dashes to represent letters?	*Morse code*
2	What does exhalation mean?	*Breathing out*
3	What happens if you cube a number?	*You multiply it by itself twice*
4	What does a mycologist study?	*Fungi*
5	What name is given to the ability of an animal to conceal itself within its surroundings?	*Camouflage*
6	Cape Horn is the southern tip of which continent?	*South America*
7	A midwife would be present at which important milestone in your life?	*Your birth*
8	Which cells in the human body do not have a nucleus?	*Red blood cells*
9	What bird is used in races because of its exceptional homing ability?	*Pigeon*
10	What are the two upper chambers of the heart called?	*The atria*
11	What is the name of the wire, rod, or metal dish that sends out or receives radio signals?	*Antenna*
12	What can you tell from the rings of a tree trunk?	*The age of the tree*
13	How many minutes are there in a day?	*1,440*
14	Which planet is nearest the Earth?	*Mars*
15	Most trucks use what type of fuel?	*Diesel*

Quiz 107
Question 10

Quiz 107
Question 6

Quiz 109 Level 3

Questions

Answers

#	Question	Answer
1	What do the British call an elevator?	*A lift*
2	If a surgeon gave someone a pacemaker, what part of the body would it help?	*The heart*
3	What is a loom?	*A machine for weaving cloth*
4	What do you call an animal that can live on land or in the water?	*Amphibian*
5	Which type of tooth is used for grinding food?	*Molar*
6	How many sides has a polygon?	*3 or more (it's a many-sided figure)*
7	Which comet orbits the sun every 76 years?	*Halley's Comet*
8	What would a spider use its spinnerets for?	*Producing threads (used in webs)*
9	Which element has the chemical symbol Fe?	*Iron*
10	What is 150% of 12?	*18*
11	What process in humans starts with an ovum and ends with a fetus?	*Pregnancy*
12	Which is the odd one out: panther, cheetah, hyena, jaguar?	*Hyena (the others are all large cats)*
13	Which planet is the closest in size to Earth?	*Venus*
14	What type of vehicle would have a derailleur?	*A bicycle (it is a type of chain)*
15	How does a python kill its prey?	*By crushing it*

Quiz 110
Question 10

Quiz 110
Question 6

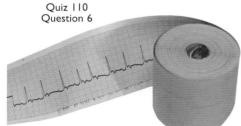

Quiz 110
Question 3

Quiz 110 Level 3

Questions

Answers

		Question	Answer
1		What type of instrument uses two or more lenses to make small objects appear much larger?	*Microscope*
2	$\sqrt{x}$	A famous government building in Washington is named after a mathematical shape. What is it?	*The Pentagon*
3		What in the body are the *rectus abdominus* and *deltoid* examples of?	*Muscles*
4		What type of medical professional performs root canal treatments?	*A dentist*
5		What is the chemical symbol of Zinc?	*Zn*
6		What name is given to the graphic recording of the electrical changes in the heart?	*ECG (electrocardiogram)*
7		Which raw material is most plastic made from?	*Oil*
8		What is the Earth's closest neighbor in space?	*The Moon*
9		What did Ladislao Biro invent in 1933?	*The ballpoint pen*
10		What kind of creature uses a "trap-door" to catch its prey?	*A trap-door spider*
11	$\sqrt{x}$	If an insect flaps its wings 30 times a second, how many times will it flap in 2 minutes?	*3,600*
12		What job does a clutch do on a car?	*It separates the gears*
13		Which are your incisors?	*The flat front teeth*
14		What black and white creature is of the genus *Equus*?	*Zebra*
15		What machine can vary its density to travel underwater or on the water's surface?	*A submarine or submersible*

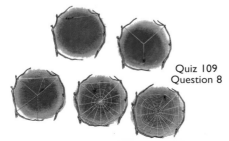

Quiz 109
Question 8

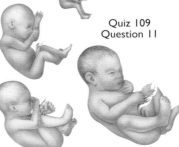

Quiz 109
Question 11

Quiz 111 Level 3

Questions

Answers

		Question	Answer
1		Which mammal is the only one that can fly?	*A bat*
2		What broadcast radio waveband operates from 160-225 kHz	*Long wave*
3		What job does bile perform in the body?	*It helps digest food*
4		What type of insect makes huge mounds more than 6 feet tall?	*Termites*
5		What does a botanist study?	*Plants*
6		Which is the world's largest desert?	*The Sahara*
7		How many sides does a parallelogram have?	*Four*
8		Barbary apes live in only one small part of Europe. Where is it?	*Gibraltar*
9		Who invented the jet engine?	*Frank Whittle*
10		What is the square root of 121?	*11*
11		If a doctor recommends taking insulin regularly, from which disease is the patient suffering?	*Diabetes*
12		About 95% of the body's calcium is found in which two areas?	*Teeth and bones*
13		Which instrument displays the change in electrical voltages over time?	*Oscilloscope*
14		What does the "N" stand for on a car's transmission?	*Neutral*
15		What was the name of the first space probe to send back pictures of Venus?	**Venera**

Quiz 112
Question 1

Quiz 112
Question 8

Quiz 112 Level 3

Questions

1. What name is given to the fertilization of plants by animals?
2. What happens to your heart rate as you grow older?
3. How many meters are there in 5.5 km?
4. What do the British call the trunk of a car?
5. What does a thermometer measure?
6. What made the craters on the moon?
7. Urine is 95% water: true or false?
8. What kind of lizard, with a long tongue, is renowned for its color-changing abilities?
9. Fireworks were invented by people living in which country?
10. Which vitamin found in liver and green vegetables, helps with clotting blood?
11. True or false: birds are the only animals with feathers?
12. Ancient scientists believed that there were only four elements: earth, fire, air, and what else?
13. What is 50% of 122?
14. What is nausea?
15. How big is one nanometer?

Answers

1. *Animal pollination*
2. *It slows down*
3. *5,500*
4. *The boot*
5. *Temperature*
6. *Meteorites*
7. *True*
8. *Chameleon*
9. *China*
10. *Vitamin K*
11. *True*
12. *Water*
13. *61*
14. *The feeling that you need to be sick*
15. *One billionth of a meter*

Quiz 111
Question 1

Quiz 111
Question 4

Quiz 113 Level 3

Questions

Answers

		Questions	Answers
1		What is plasma?	*The liquid part of blood*
2		Which is usually bigger—a gulf or a bay?	*A gulf*
3		In which war were the first jet planes used?	*World War II*
4		What does biodegradable mean?	*Able to rot away naturally*
5		Which part of the body is affected by conjunctivitus?	*The eye*
6		What paper is used to measure acids and alkalis?	*Litmus paper*
7		What ape shares its name with the inventor of the heart-lung machine?	*Gibbon*
8		How many decades are there in a millennium?	*100*
9		What is the other name for a typhoon?	*Hurricane*
10		Which is larger, a destroyer or a battleship?	*A battleship*
11		What are the names of the three segments of a bee?	*Head, thorax, abdomen*
12		Biology is the study of what?	*Living things*
13		Which term describes half of the diameter of a circle?	*The radius*
14		What type of food plant do the British call aubergine?	*Eggplant*
15		What word describes a region's average weather over a long period of time?	*Its climate*

Quiz 114
Question 11

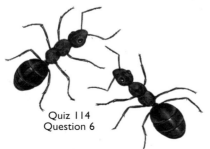

Quiz 114
Question 6

Quiz 114
Question 8